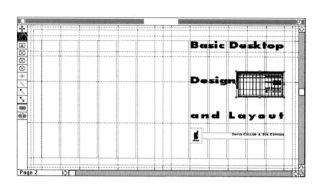

Page 2

Basic Desktop

Design

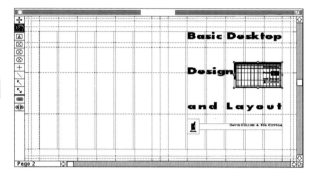

and Layout

NORTH LIGHT BOOKS

Cincinnati, Ohio

DAVID COLLIER & BOB COTTON

A QUARTO BOOK

Copyright © 1989 Quarto Publishing plc
First published in the U.S.A. by
North Light Books, an imprint of
F & W Publications, Inc
1507 Dana Avenue
Cincinnati, Ohio 45207

ISBN 0-89134-285-0

This book was designed and produced by
Quarto Publishing plc
The Old Brewery
6 Blundell Street
London N7 9BH

Senior Editor Susanna Clarke
Editor Carol Hupping

Designer David Collier
Picture Researcher Valya Alexander
Photographer Michael Taylor

Art Director Moira Clinch
Editorial Director Carolyn King

Special thanks to Brian Cookman and Ingrid Clifford

Manufactured in Hong Kong by Regent Publishing Services Ltd
Printed in Hong Kong by South Sea International Press Ltd

Contents

Introduction

You are reading this book because you've decided that you want to optimize your investment in desktop publishing (DTP) – to get more out of your computer system in terms of quality and in terms of the enjoyment it gives you – both of these are valid reasons for learning more about good graphic design.

GOOD DESIGN – WHY BOTHER ?

If you are not a graphic designer and know little or nothing about type or typefaces, what difference has this made in your ability to follow an author's argument, or in your enjoyment of reading since you were a child? Has your lack of typographic knowledge affected the ability of the author to communicate with you through his printed words? Many people would say that graphic design matters not at all; indeed, there is no scientific evidence that the use of one text typeface or another has the slightest effect on our comprehension of the content of the text. So why bother to design reading material at all?

People who say it doesn't matter have perhaps never realized that all printed material, be it well or badly designed, is nevertheless designed by someone. Indeed, most of us are, thankfully, only rarely exposed to bad design. All the books and magazines, all the adverts, posters, record sleeves, soup can labels, cigarette packets – everything we might come into contact with that has been printed – has been subject to the design process. Over the years, although you've probably given it little thought, you have been the ultimate target of a multi-million dollar industry – an industry devoted to considering every last detail of the design of every printed item. The books you have read will have been typeset in such a way, with a type that has been carefully chosen for its readability, that you need never have noticed the actual typeface used. Whether you are reading a novel, or the copy of an advert, if it's good, design never gets in the way of an author's message.

DESIGN AND COMMUNICATION

But good graphic design is more than the uninitiated not noticing the design at all. Good design will enhance the communication of an idea, both by attracting us to look at it in the first place and then by presenting the content to us in such a way that the ideas that are embodied in it come over to us in a series of carefully graded, that is, carefully designed, steps.

This aspect of graphic design – the appraisal and presentation of content using a logical and appropriate method – is one that is central to efficient communication and forms the basis of much modern design practice. As such, it is the ideal approach for a newcomer to design and provides a good basis from which to develop a suitable design. However, many designers see this approach as a style in its own right, a style very much associated with the Modern Movement in graphics (the period from around 1920 to 1960). Such designers feel that graphics should also be more attractive, more fashionable and more eclectic in the range of visual and cultural references that it includes.

GRAPHICS AND FASHION

Graphics, like all aspects of design, has always been affected to some extent by fashion, and because designers are conscious of the style of the times they are living in, many naturally reflect this style in their work. Indeed, many printed items are designed to appeal directly to a fashion- and style-conscious audience and demand the very latest graphic trends in order to stay competitive. If you want to design in these areas you must train yourself to be acutely aware of the shifts in graphic fashion, and to do this you must first study the recent history of graphics. Like fashions in clothes, graphic design is constantly referring back to its past history, reinterpreting styles from previous periods and marrying them with what is new in today's world.

THE NEW WORLD OF DTP

It has always been the case in the history of printing that new technology offers new opportunities in type and image origination and processing, and fresh inspiration for the designer. What is new in graphics today is of course the whole field of computer graphics, of which DTP is a substantial part. The technology we now use for image making and typographic design is responsible for a vast range of new visual effects – effects that were impossible to produce a few years ago.

The combination of fashion and technological influences produces new styles – and quite naturally engenders reactions to these styles – and it is this interplay that acts to constantly rejuvenate design, allowing each generation to formulate a style of expression peculiarly its own. Whether it is in the height of fashion or consciously reflecting the style of an earlier period, good graphic design enhances the communication of ideas by presenting information clearly, in a style that the reader or viewer finds attractive.

Elements of Desktop Design

The process of designing for graphics involves several stages, from the original idea that some printed work is required, through the various stages of roughs and artwork, to the finished, printed job. Over the next few pages, we will consider all these stages in some detail, starting with the actual process of design.

SETTING UP THE JOB

The original idea for a printed piece of work may come from you – it may be a personal letterhead, or a visiting card – or it may come from another source – someone who approaches you and asks if you will design them (for example) a range of stationery. We will call this person – whether they are paying you or not – the client. Most designers will approach such a graphic design job in the following way.

ASSESSING THE CLIENT'S NEEDS

Clients may have a very clear idea of what they want done. It is the designer's task to translate this idea into a visually clear graphic statement. If the client's requirements are vague, or imprecise, then the designer must suggest a range of options, perhaps with some estimate of potential costs.

The client wants a range of stationery. What exactly does he want? Stationery might include a letterhead, a visiting card, an envelope – and if the client is in business – an invoice, a bill, a business card, a range of large and small size envelopes, and perhaps sticky labels for parcels. These requirements should be listed and included in the job specification.

Then you must carefully note the details of what the client wants printed on each item of stationery. Letterheads might include the following: client's name (or company name), address, telephone number, FAX number, Telex number, list of officers (president, vice president etc), and perhaps a logotype or trademark.Business cards may include just the client's name, or company name, phone number and address, and so on.

Determine what the budget for the job is - including both your own fee as the designer, and the budget for print. This will often determine the printing process, and in turn, the way you prepare the artwork you will need.

In addition to his material requirements, it is essential that you know the answers to some of the following questions, which will help you begin to formulate your design solution:

- What stationery is the client already using, if any?
- How far does this present stationery go in meeting his needs (both now and in the immediate future)?
- What sort of image does he want the new stationery to project?
  (For example, a lawyer might want to project a very different image to that of a rock musician, or a photographer.)
- How does this image compare with the stationery his competition (or peer group) is using?
- What sort of people (friends? customers? colleagues?) will be in receipt of this new stationery? (Remember that graphic design is often the intermediary between the client and his customers, and it's important for the designer to build up a picture of both).

FORMULATION OF A BRIEF

When the objective has been clarified, a written brief should be prepared and agreed by both client and designer. The brief should specify what is to be done, the agreed fee, the deadline, and an agreement as to a possible rejection fee (if the client decides not to go ahead after the designer has prepared roughs and presentation visuals). The brief should be specific and inclusive - the more detailed the job specification the less chance there is of any (expensive!) misunderstandings later in the design and print process.

DESIGN AS THE SOLUTION TO A PROBLEM

We can consider that the process of graphic design involves the designer in defining the client's needs (his problem), and inventing a solution - the finished design that answers all the client's requirements. When you are in possession of all the necessary information outlined above, how do you convert this information into a piece of good graphic design? Next, we'll briefly outline the background experience that the designer brings to a design job.

DESIGN SKILLS AND THE DESIGNER'S BACKGROUND EXPERIENCE

The sort of skills and knowledge that a designer acquires during his training and professional life include the ability to draw (not necessarily be a great illustrator or artist, but to draw well enough to be able to think on paper – sketching ideas in sometimes a very rough and ready way); a knowledge of color (in illustration and in print); a knowledge of a variety of typefaces (their characteristics, and mode of use); a knowledge of illustration styles and techniques; of photography (how to take, print, edit and crop a photograph); skills in the preparation of artwork (being clean, tidy and precise!); a knowledge of printing processes; and, perhaps as important as any of these, the ability to objectively appraise a problem and logically (and intuitively) work out the solution. But don't be dismayed by this long list. If you're visually committed enough to acquire a DTP system, or enjoy working with it, then these skills can be acquired gradually, as and when you feel you need to have them.

For example, in our stationery design job we need to know only about the typefaces we have available in our laserprinter and about the range of layout options we have in the page makeup program we are using. Some experimentation with these, in a variety of layouts and styles, will help you build up a knowledge of their characteristics. Remember that any information will fall into a hierarchy of importance. On a letterhead, it may well be that the client's name will take precedence over the address, the address over the telephone number or company officers, and so on. Your choice of typeface, style and point size should reflect this hierarchy.

In addition to this information, study examples of other designers' work – most libraries will have annuals of prize-winning graphics, often classified to include a section on stationery (look in the house style or corporate identity sections as well). From your research, some notion of the general graphic style that is needed for the stationery will emerge.

THUMBNAILS

With this background you will now be in a position to sketch out the graphic possibilities in the form of thumbnails. Thumbnails are an ideas-generating and ideas-checking tool. Do not show thumbnails to the client unless he is used to seeing work at this level and he has a clear understanding of what thumbnails are for. (Note that most clients will not know – unless you tell them – the process you are working through to achieve your finished design. Do not confuse clients with too wide a choice of alternative approaches or with thumbnail roughs that they may have difficulty in interpreting.)

WORKING ROUGHS

From thumbnail sketches, working, full-sized roughs are prepared, where all the graphic components of the job – the type, and any illustrations, photographs, graphics, etc, are indicated in rough (generally using fiber-tip markers), so that you can assess how the initial idea will work. Choices of typefaces, sizes and layout formats, as well as style and content of illustrations and photographs, type of paper, color tints, and the final print process (if not already decided by budget) are made at this time. Printers' estimates can be sought at this stage, too.

In DTP, the working rough can be produced as a first proof of the finished job, this proof also being usually of a quality high enough for a presentation visual for the client.

PRESENTATION VISUAL

Now a visual can be presented to the client. Presentation visuals should give the client as accurate an idea as possible as to how the finished job will look. Traditionally at this stage type is hand rendered. Roughs of any illustrations and photographs are then pasted into position. The whole visual is then given an acetate overlay and shown for client approval.

In DTP, of course, the availability of laserproofs of the job – completed to client presentation stage – enable you to avoid some of these tasks (especially if the job is in black and white only), while scanned images can give the client a fairly accurate idea of how logos or illustrations will look.

ARTWORK

When the client has approved the presentation visual, or after corrections have been made, then the final artwork can be produced. In traditional terms this would involve typesetting, the preparation (or commissioning) of illustrations and photographs and then the preparation of line or halftone prints of these images, and the pasteup of all these components, ready to be photographed as camera-ready art.

In DTP the artwork stage involves making any corrections to the presentation visual file, and perhaps taking a disk copy of the job to a firm for output on a laser typesetter as final artwork.

PROOFING

Finally, printed proofs from the printers are then checked and submitted to the client for any final proofreading and corrections. The print run can then commence with duly corrected plates.

Creating Text Shapes

Just as traditional basic design education uses the manipulation of cut-out paper shapes on a sheet of paper to encourage the student to think visually, so we will use the page format of DTP software to begin our exploration of design. DTP software gives us a considerable advantage over cut-out paper in that the tool we will be using to explore basic design options is also the very same tool we will be using later to create finished designs and artwork ready for printing.

We'll begin to explore layout by conceiving of the page as a picture frame in which we will arrange some simple shapes representing text blocks. This is entirely appropriate to the graphic design process, as it is how designers begin to think about a real graphics job. We can think of these experimental layouts as thumbnails for future designs and as an introduction to visual thinking.

Page layout hinges on balance – in the placing of text blocks and in the consideration of the shapes you make with the white paper that's left around these blocks. The interaction of white space and text blocks can create a variety of effects. Look at the examples opposite. Some are static, some dynamic. Some surround the text area with white space to give a calm, peaceful effect, in others the type block is dominant, demanding our attention.

◆ CHECK**LIST**

- Think of the page as a picture frame for you to compose in.

- Keep text shapes simple at this stage.

- Balance shapes against the white space on the page.

- Try creating a dynamic text shape and a passive text shape. How do the positions of the shapes on the page help to emphasize these points?

- What effect do you think a centered text shape has?

- Try creating examples of all the text shapes in this spread.

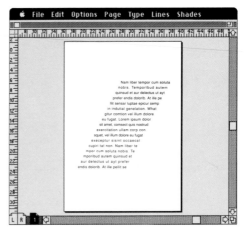

The diagonal margin is achieved by running the type around two white rules, which cannot be seen. This simple effect would have been extremely costly to produce by conventional setting, as each line would have to be given a separate indent value.

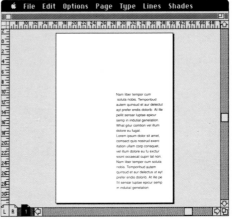

This is the righthand page of a spread. The layout would work well with a full-page photo, reversing the text out as if it were a long caption. The edge of this text shape is centered on the page, so it was decided to range the text left to lead the viewer on into the next spread.

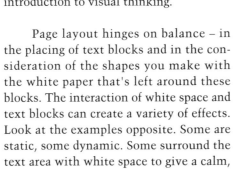

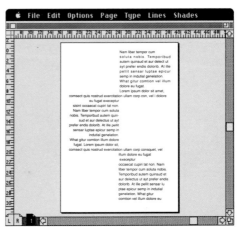

This is a layout for a catalogue, where the type echoes the layout of photos on a facing page. Note how the blocks are not separated – they each have a run in of one shared line. This layout was created by using invisible blocks to force the text runaround. Having one line in common helps prevent uneven line spacing.

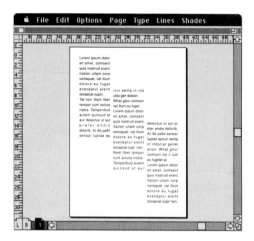

These three text blocks are all of equal length. To find this length, the whole story was run as a single column over a number of pages, then the total length was divided by three. The boxes were staggered down the page to create a more interesting effect.

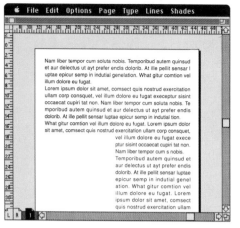

This block of text balances on a thin support, in contrast to the gravity rule, which says that type has weight and should be arranged according to gravity, building up text blocks from the bottom of the page.

Shaping the text into this arc was done by drawing a graphic of the outer half of the arc and importing it into the DTP program. A circle was drawn with the DTP program itself for the inner circle. Both elements were then made "invisible runarounds" so the type would follow their shape, yet the elements themselves would not appear in the printout.

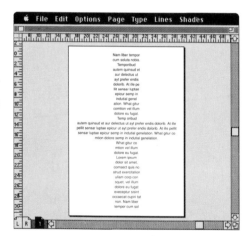

This cross shape could have been created in two ways: by pulling the text into three rectangular text blocks or by leaving the text as one large block and placing rectangular "invisible runarounds" in each corner. The second technique is much better, as you avoid all the problems of uneven leading when you flow text from one block to another.

This hexagon could have been created using four invisible rules but a quicker method is to draw a graphic diamond and import it. The text doesn't start right at the top of the diamond; if it did it would cause ugly hyphenation as the program attempted to make one- and two-letter words.

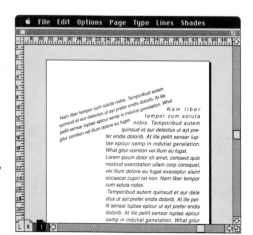

Angling text is currently impossible within reliable DTP packages, but it is achievable by setting text in a drawing program. However to get the margin on the text to be vertical, spaces had to be manually inserted at the beginning of each line. An alternative would be to set the text from a DTP package with a diagonal margin and physically cut out and rotate the text by hand.

Introducing Picture Shapes

When we combine text and picture blocks, the basic design considerations – of balance and the use of white space – are the same. But now we have another factor to consider – the additional tonal quality of the image block. The tone of a block is defined by the ratio of black:white that it contains – the more black, the darker the tone and the heavier the effect. Blocks of different tones will have the effect of different weights on the page, and these must be balanced with each other as well as against the white spaces.

Balance is more difficult to achieve in dynamic asymmetrical layouts, where you must consider more carefully the white space left on the page. Many of the innovations of modern graphic design stemmed from designers who thought of page layout as a structure of text blocks that must balance and support each other, rather like the components of a building.

Consider carefully how each separate block relates to the others, and to the edges of the page. Our sample layouts appear solidly fixed into the page, drawing their solidity from being anchored to a side, corner, center line, or to the top or bottom edges. Text blocks should not float free on the page, but should be supported by at least one element that ties them to the page edge.

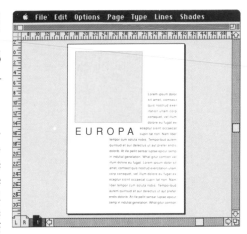

By indenting the picture into the text it is immediately made clear which text to read to get more information about the photo. The indentation works as a pointer, inviting the reader to the text.

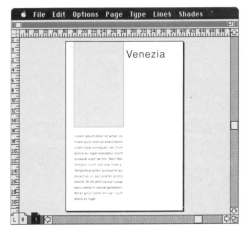

The size and position of the text block echoes the shape of the photo and balances it across an imaginary central horizontal axis.

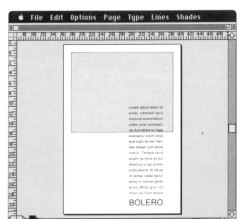

The type starts from within the photo and continues outside it. When applying this technique, be sure your photo is composed in such a way that type and image will not interfere. This is a good technique when you have an extra long caption, establishing a direct connection between text and image.

◆ CHECK**LIST**

- Try moving the image block and the text shape around; see how this affects the balance of the page.

- Think of the size of the blocks as reflecting their weight. This can help to achieve a visual balance.

- What effect does a small image block have when set against a large text block?

- Try bleeding image blocks from the edge of the page.

- What effect do the ragged edges of ranged-right, ranged-left and centered text blocks have against the rectangular page?

Bleeding a picture from the top of the page creates a modern feel. This is because in the old days of letterpress printing a large "grip" was needed at the top of the page. (This could be avoided by printing the whole publication upside down, but who'd think of doing that?)

Runarounds are extremely simple to create with most DTP packages. This circular runaround was created by drawing a circle, making it white and defining it as a text runaround object.

Using photos very small looks great, especially for colored slides: a concentrated burst of information! It also allows very spacious, stylish layouts to be created with plenty of white space to frame the page contents.

This dynamic arrangement of small squared photos is interesting, while adhering to a strict grid.

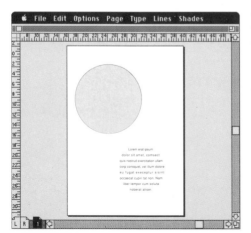

Text has been set within a circle here to echo the shape of this fisheye lens photograph. The circles are different sizes to avoid monotony.

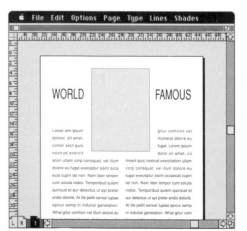

This two-column grid is neatly broken by a photograph at the top of the page. The photograph allows the text to start slightly further down the page without giving the appearance of a hole.

Thinking About Type

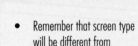

The designer's job is to take the author's text, choose a suitable typeface and typesize for it, and then to lay the typeset text out on the page. As a DTP operator, you will already know how text is typeset and positioned on the page. However, you know that there's more to it than just knowing the techniques involved. In fact, as you work through the remainder of this book, not only will you realize that there are more sophisticated levels of typesetting technique to be learned, but also that typography is as much about design as it is about technique. So what is typographic design?

Design combines thinking and seeing, using your brain, hands and eyes to manipulate and experiment with your materials. Everyone can think, but many of us have lost the natural ability to think visually. The purpose of these basic exercises is to get you to think visually again. To do this we are also going to find out more about type, so that we can judge the effect it can have on the page.

Typography deals with typefaces, and to begin to design successfully with type we have to know the variety of typefaces available; how they are measured, classified and spaced; which types are suitable for which jobs; and how they look on the page.

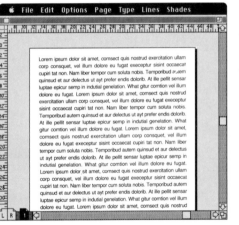

When setting long passages, leading (the space between lines of type) can greatly affect the appeal of a page. If type is set too tight it looks too black and dense for easy reading.

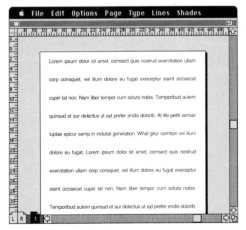

In most typefaces, the linespacing should be about 120% of the body size (for example, 10 point type with 12 point leading). This is the default (automatic) leading available in most DTP programs.

Many other factors will decide the optimum leading. For instance, with a relatively short passage you can add a lot of leading to achieve an aesthetically pleasing effect.

Lorem ipsum dolor sit amet, comsect quis nostrud exercit ation ullam corp consquet, vel illum dolore eu fugat exece ptur sisint occaecat cupiri tat non. Nam liber tempor cum soluta nobis. Temporibud autem quinsud et aur delectus ut ayt prefer endis dolorib. At ille pellit sensar luptae epicur semp in indutial genelation. What gitur comtion vel illum dolore eu fugat. Lorem ipsum dolor sit amet, comsect quis nostrud exercitation ullam corp consquet, vel illum dolore eu fugat execeptur sisint occaecat cupiri tat non. Nam liber te mpor cum soluta nobis. Temporibud autem quinsud et aur delectus ut ayt prefer endis dolorib. At ille pellit sensar luptae epicur semp in indutial genelation. What gitur comtion vel illum dolore eu fugat. Lorem ipsum dolor sit amet, comsect quis nostrud exercitation ullam corp consquet, vel illum dolore eu fugat execeptur sisint occaecat cupiri tat non. Nam liber tempor cum soluta nobis. Temporibud autem quinsud et aur delectus ut ayt prefer endis dolorib. At ille pellit sensar luptae epicur semp in indutial genelation. What gitur comtion vel illum dolore eu fugat. Lorem ipsum dolor sit amet, co msect quis nostrud exercitation ullam corp consquet, vel illum dolore eu fugat execeptur sisint occaecat cupiri tat non. Nam liber tempor cum soluta nobis.

The example here and the one below show exactly the same point size of type on exactly the same leading. All that has changed is the font itself, and you can see how this significantly affects the tone of the page. The top example is a sans serif face, Helvetica.

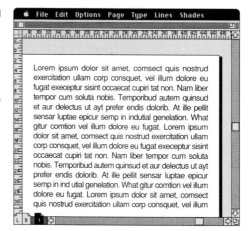

Letterspacing between characters will greatly affect the gray value of a page. This passage of text has a small amount of negative spacing, and it looks crammed.

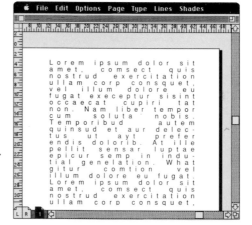

As well as affecting the gray value of type, adding letterspacing will obviously affect the length of a passage. This passage is almost illegible because of unthoughtfully applied letterspacing.

Lorem ipsum dolor sit amet, comsect quis nostrud exerc itation ullam corp consquet, vel illum dolore eu fugat ex eceptur sisint occaecat cupiri tat non. Nam liber tempor cum soluta nobis. Temporibud autem quinsud et aur dele ctus ut ayt prefer endis dolorib. At ille pellit sensar luptae epicur semp in indutial genelation. What gitur comtion vel illum dolore eu fugat. Lorem ipsum dolor sit amet, co msect quis nostrud exercitation ullam corp consquet, vel illum dolore eu fugat execeptur sisint occaecat cupiri tat non. Nam liber tempor cum soluta nobis. Temporibud autem quinsud et aur delectus ut ayt prefer endis dolorib. At ille pellit sensar luptae epicur semp in indutial genel ation. What gitur comtion vel illum dolore eu fugat. Lorem ipsum dolor sit amet, comsect quis nostrud exercitation ullam.corp consquet, vel illum dolore eu fugat execeptur sisint occaecat cupiri tat non. Nam liber tempor cum soluta nobis. Temporibud autem quinsud et aur delectus ut ayt prefer endis dolorib. At ille pellit sensar luptae epicur semp in indutial genelation. What gitur comtion vel illum dolore eu fugat. Lorem ipsum dolor sit amet, comsect quis nostrud exercitation ullam corp consquet, vel illum dolore eu fugat execeptur sisint occaecat cupiri tat non. Nam liber tempor cum soluta nobis.

This example is Times-Roman, a well-known serif face. Note that different fonts of the same point size may appear to differ in their actual size.

With increased letterspacing you should also add leading so that the eye is drawn to the next character, not to the next line down. More spacing should be added between words than between characters.

Legibility and Readability

The two words legibility and readability are often confused. Legibility refers to the clarity of the type character – how well each character is defined and easily identified. Readability describes how some typefaces are suitable for long texts meant for continuous reading.

A typeface may be legible but not very readable, as for instance many of the teletext bitmapped faces. They are legible at the size they are used on the TV screen, but they would be unsuitable for long texts. So legibility and readability are not synonymous qualities!

Different types of graphic applications require different degrees of legibility. For example a road sign needs to be legible at a great distance, but postage stamp design may be illegible at arm's length. The degree of legibility required in any graphic design will depend on what the design is for, who will be reading it, and when and where it will be read. Conditions may determine the need for large neon lettering, fluorescent ink or 6 point type, all depending upon the purpose and function of the job.

Display type will have to be legible (so that it is noticeable!), but text type will have to be both legible and readable. Remember that we read text in groups of words at a time, and it is the shapes made by the characters viewed together that enables the reader to easily interpret these groups.

When dealing with type in detail, it's good to have an understanding of how people read it. Readers are most likely to see a full word or groups of words at a time, using the shapes of ascenders and descenders (the parts of letters that fall above and below the line) and the counters (the white holes inside letters) to aid recognition.

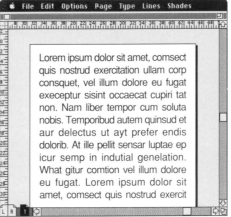
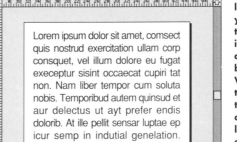

This paragraph of text has even letterspacing. When you enlarge a typeface drastically, it is usual to reduce the amount of spacing between characters. Vice versa for small type, where it is usual to add a small amount of letterspacing. Be careful not to overlap characters.

This paragraph has been substantially letterspaced, or tracked, as it is known in conventional typesetting when applied to a paragraph of text. This doesn't help readability on body text, as the word shapes that help people read can become disguised.

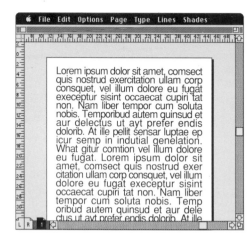

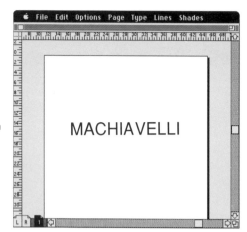

Leading also helps readability. When there is not enough spacing between lines, ascenders and descenders clash and confuse the words. Also the reader's eye may skip a line. Leading helps create a strong horizontal guideline for the eye.

Certain character pairs need to be overlapped to look right, such as "T" and "o." This is called kerning, which most DTP programs automatically control. In this example automatic kerning has been turned off, resulting in a visually uneven space between the "A" and "V."

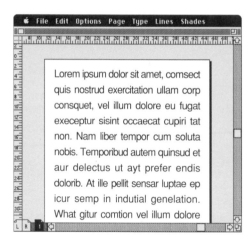

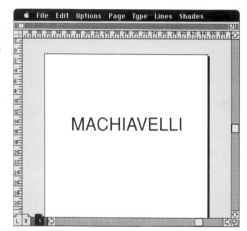

Optimum leading is affected by line length as well as the amount of copy. Be careful not to add too much leading to long passages, as this can cause the same line to be read twice.

Automatic kerning has been applied in this example, which resulted in the "A" and "V" being closed together. In some large headlines you may wish to manually kern certain characters, which most DTP packages will allow you to do.

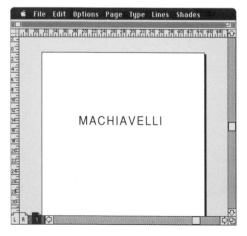

Certain methods of emphasizing words can diminish readability. Setting a paragraph in all capitals disguises the word shapes.

This example cheats! To avoid manual kerning, an amount of letterspacing was added between all characters, covering up any relatively small discrepancies between certain pairs.

Type Size and Measure

Type is measured in points (there are approximately 72 points to an inch). There are two major classifications of size that relate to what type is used for: Display type, which is type set at sizes over about 14 point for headlines, titles, etc, and Text type, which is set under 14 point and generally at 9-12 point, which is used for passages of text. Text type has to be easily readable over long passages, and it has to be highly legible if it is used for timetables or lists of parts that are designed for intermittent reading.

The space between lines of type is called leading (pronounced ledding). As leading is measured from baseline to baseline (ie from the bottom of a capital letter on one line to the bottom of a capital letter on the line above), the measurement includes the point size of the type. For example, 10 point type set with 12 point leading (or 10/12, or ten on twelve) means that there will be two points of leading between each line of type.

Leading can affect both the readability and the legibility of text type. If there is no leading, then the eye can find it very difficult to scan along the line, since there is no strong horizontal band of white space to guide it. If there is too much leading, the eye is swamped with white space. Both extremes make reading long passages of text a very tiring experience.

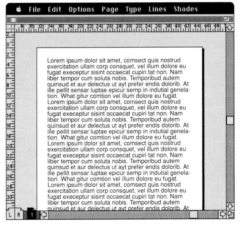

This page of comfortably sized and generously leaded type makes for easy reading. It would ideally be complemented by using a serif font.

This is the same passage but set in a larger point size with less leading. Note how the reduction in leading makes the text more difficult to read and makes it appear crammed tightly together.

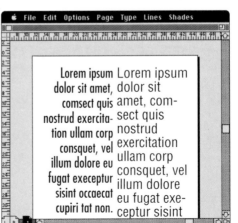

When leading is set to auto on your system, lines of type will be set with the amount of leading that the manufacturer has programmed into the software. On auto leading different typefaces at the same point size will not necessarily have the same leading. This should be borne in mind when aligning columns, and the leading should be specified.

Lorem ipsum dolor sit amet, comsect quis nostrud exercitation ullam corp consquet, vel illum dolore eu fugat execeptur sisint occaecat cupiri tat non. Nam liber tempor cum soluta nobis. Temporibud autem quinsud et aur delectus ut ayt prefer endis dolorib. At ille pellit sensar luptae epicur semp in indutial genelation. What gitur comtion temp vel illum dolore eu fugat.

Lorem ipsum dolor sit amet, comsect quis nostrud exercitation ullam corp consquet, vel illum dolore eu fugat execeptur sisint occaecat cupiri tat non. Nam liber tempor cum soluta nobis. Temporibud autem quinsud et aur comtion vel illum dolore eu fugat. Lorem ipsum dolor sit amet, comsect quis nostrud exercitation ullam corp consquet, vel illum dolore eu fugat execeptur sisint occaecat cupiri tat non. Nam liber tempor cum soluta nobis. Temporibud autem quinsud et aur delectus ut ayt prefer endis dolorib. At ille pellit sensar luptae epicur semp in .

Ut ayt prefer endis dolorib. At ille pellit sensar luptae epicur semp in indutial genelation. What gitur comtion vel illum dolore eu fugat. Lorem ipsum dolor sit amet, comsect quis nostrud exercitation ullam corp consquet, vel illum dolore delectus ut

ayt prefer endis dolorib. At ille pellit sensar luptae epicur semp in indutial genelation. What gitur comtion vel illum dolore eu fugat. Lorem ipsum dolor sit amet, comsect quis nostrud exercitation ullam corp consquet, tempor cum soluta nobis. Temporibud autem quinsud et aur delectus ut ayt prefer endis dolorib. At ille pellit tu dolor sit amet, cum sensar luptae epicur.

What gitur comtion vel illum dolore eu fugat. Lorem ipsum dolor sit execeptur sisint occaecat

cupiri tat non. Nam liber tempor cum soluta nobis. Temporibud autem quinsud et aur delectus ut ayt prefer endis dolorib. At ille pellit sensar luptae epicur semp in indutial genelation. What gitur comtion vel illum dolore

Here we can see the effect of using different sized type on three different measures. In the top example the larger type with generous leading works well over a long measure, but the eye would tire reading the smaller type. In the middle example the larger type is still very readable and over this length would be suitable for a caption or a heading on an advertisement. Over this measure the smaller type also works. In the bottom example the measure is too short for the large type but is an ideal column width for the smaller type.

How to Emphasize Words

Type is organized into families of related styles, or variants. We can use these variants to add emphasis to parts of the text. The most useful are bold and italic, both of which stress the word or phrase so treated. The italic style, with its connotation of handwriting, is also suited to quotations. Underlining is an ugly hangover from mechanical typewriters and is best avoided.

Apart from variants, we can use settings in all capital letters, small caps (that are the same size as the lowercase letter x of the normal typeface), or extra large caps (perhaps two or three times the point size of the normal text face).

The main issue here is not which variants you use, but how many different ones you may use in a complete passage of text and how often you use them. Emphatic points become irritating if there are too many of them, and doubly irritating if there is too much variation in the style of emphasis. Decide when and in what situation you are going to use a bold or italic variant, then stick to this rule throughout. Similarly with quotes, divide not only the style of emphasis that you will use, but also the amount of indenting in the layout.

◆ CHECK**LIST**

- Use bold and italic variants of your text typeface for emphasizing words.

- Bold emphasis is effective but affects readability.

- Italic emphasis is more subtle and doesn't affect readability.

- Establish a set of rules for your treatment of emphasis so that the different types of emphasis are used consistently.

- How many methods of emphasis are there in the particular job?

- Overuse of emphasis is irritating and counterproductive.

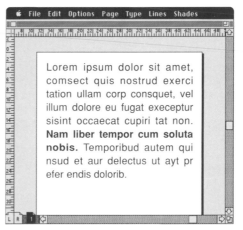

There are various ways to pick out and emphasize words within a passage. Making words bold is the simplest way to make a piece of text stand out from a distance and attract the eye of a casual reader. However it jars slightly and tends to stop the reader's eye as it scans along the line.

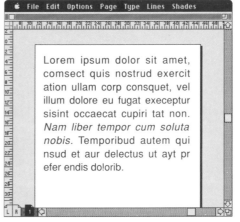

Making a word italic is a more subtle way of emphasizing a point. This technique is much more flowing, and it allows readers to comfortably continue reading the passage, while still making the words stand out in their minds. However italic words will not jump off the page as much as emboldened ones do.

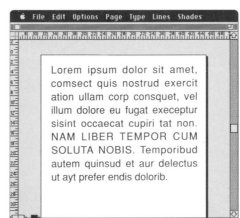

Picking a sentence out in all capital letters serves to make a clear statement. Usually this is used to reinforce instructions, but it can cause your setting to look more like a typed manuscript than something professionally typeset.

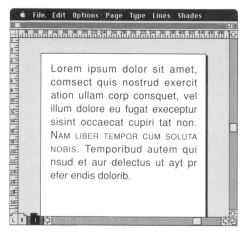

Small capitals are scaled-down versions of capital letters. These provide a classy and distinctive type-style available directly from the keyboard in most DTP applications. They are often used in first lines of new stories or for real names, but they can be used to stress a whole sentence if necessary.

Here a couple of words have been picked out extra large. This looks good in this example because the rest of the characters have been set with plenty of leading. However you may find you don't often have the space to use such a device.

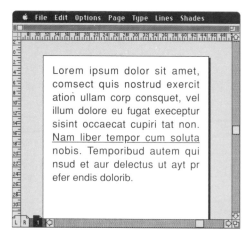

Underlining of words is a hangover from the days of the mechanical typewriter and in most cases should be avoided.

Converse to the technique of highlighting words in bold, here two words have been put into a lighter tint. This might normally have the effect of causing them to recede, but due to their very difference, they stand out. This technique will only work with extremely bold typefaces that are fat enough to be legible on a gray screen.

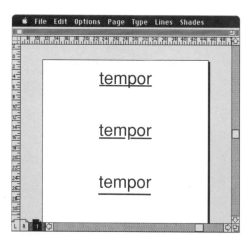

The danger is that the rule will slice through a descender as in the top example. If you feel a heading has to be underlined, you should draw a proper rule and be careful to leave consistent space around any descenders as in the middle example. Or leave sufficient space between the type and rule as shown in the bottom example.

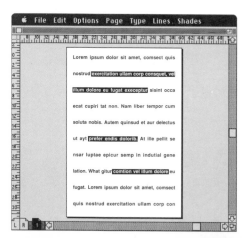

Setting a few words white out of black is one of the most effective highlighting techniques. However, due to the way most DTP programs work, with reversed-out text being composed of two elements (the white text and the black block), it is usually too time-consuming a procedure for body text.

Shapes made by Text

The simplest of layouts involve only simple rectangular blocks of text, but with a little extra attention many more shapes are possible.

Rectangular blocks of text are made by justifying – that is, spacing out each line of type so that it fills the required measure (the maximum length of text line). This is done automatically; the page makeup software adds white spaces between words to vertically align both the lefthand and righthand edges of the text block, giving it a strong rectilinear shape. The rectangle echoes the shape of the page, and because it leaves rectilinear white space around it, can simplify the task of layout.

Text ranged-left creates a straight edge down the lefthand side of the text block and a ragged righthand edge. This is perhaps the most readable of all the text layout options because word spacing is even and consistent throughout the text, and lines of type end naturally, the line breaking on a word space, not in the middle of a word.

Centered text blocks are ragged down both edges and create a surrounding white space that is symmetrical and non-rectilinear. The natural balance of centered text lends it an air of formal authority.

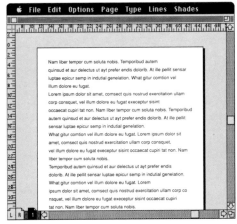

Straightforward justified text: to break up the grayness of a block, various devices can be used to separate paragraphs (or even sentences). Here the first line of each paragraph has been indented. Conventionally the indent should be an even multiple of the leading (ie, 12 point type should have a 12 or 24 point indent).

The advantage of ranged-left text such as this is that none of the spaces between words or characters will be distorted in order to force justification. This makes it ideal for text set over a short measure.

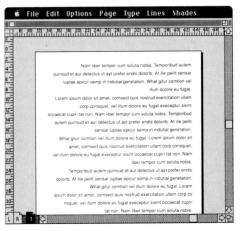

Ranged-right, or ragged-left text is more difficult to read than standard ranged-left because the eye has to search for the beginnings of lines.

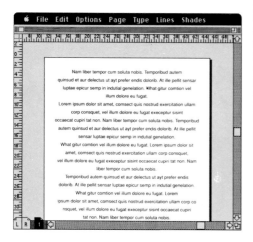

Conventional centered text is usually associated with classical layouts. It works well when there is only one column of text on a page but should be used carefully in multiple-column layouts.

The overhanging paragraph beginnings here are called hanging indents. They are excellent for separating paragraphs in an immediately visible way. However this format needs a whole column to be left empty for the indent to hang into. If you've got the space, it can be very effective.

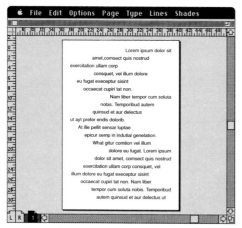

These lines are of equal length but have been moved horizontally. Called staggered justification, it was done totally on-screen, but often this effect is most easily achieved by cutting up a printed passage of ordinary text. Being able to match conventional techniques with hi-tech allows many more possibilities than just the computer alone can offer.

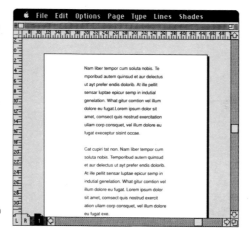

Paragraph gaps are typical of modern publications and even business letters, where the gap has virtually replaced the indent. If you are using this technique in multiple-column layouts, the gap should be an even multiple of the leading (ie, if you have 12 point leading, the gap should be 12 or 24 points).

This is another effect only really achievable when the designer controls the typeset-ting equipment directly. To force text into this shape two rules had to be drawn. The text was forced to flow around them, and the size of the type and the triangle formed by the rules were adjusted until an acceptable composition was achieved.

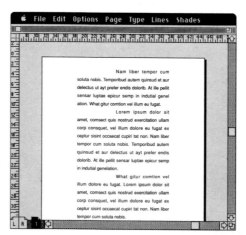

Large indents often cause a page of text to look uneven because some para-graph endings fall short of the beginning of the next line. This can give the appear-ance of extra line spacing between paragraphs and should be avoided.

Organizing Your Page/1

In order to establish a visual continuity throughout a single publication, or throughout a series of related graphic jobs (such as a series of ads), designers use a layout plan called a grid. The grid marks the position of margins and text columns with vertical and horizontal guide lines so that text blocks occupy the same relative position on each page. Grids are derived from initial thumbnails and rough sketches and must relate to the function of the design.

Generally, printed material is designed to be used either for continuous reading (as textbooks, novels, etc), or for intermittent reading (magazines, reference works, catalogues, timetables, etc). This mode of use implies a physical difference in how it is made, its scale and the disposition of text material on the pages. For example, reference works are often large and bulky, like encyclopedias, and are designed to be used opened out on a table or desk, whereas novels are held in the hand, supported behind by the fingers, and held by the thumb which is positioned at the lower end of the inside margin. Because these two books will be used differently, their text material will most likely be laid out differently. A novel may need a larger bottom and inside margin, for example.

The examples here demonstrate the layout possibilities of a simple one-column grid. Consider the effect of varying the size of the margins and their relative proportions.

CHECK**LIST**

- Grid design is based on a thorough analysis of the graphic problem and is developed from thumbnail roughs of the layout.

- Grids indicate the position of text blocks, images, titles, subheadings, etc.

- Grids enable the designer to establish a visual unity throughout a particular job.

- Consider how the grid allows for a binding margin, for pagination, for headers and footers, etc.

- Experiment with page margins: the successful grid will relate harmoniously to the paper size and orientation.

- Try working in pica measure rather than millimeters or inches; typefaces use the pica measure.

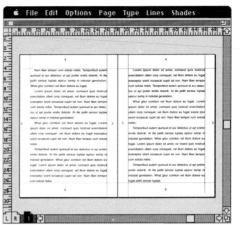

This double-page spread shows some classic proportions for margins (represented by the numbers). The bottom (foot) margin is considerably larger to overcome the optical illusion of "slippage" (where an image seems to optically slip downward in a frame unless it has an increased foot margin).

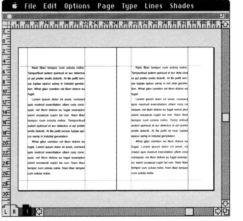

This is an example of an asymmetrical grid. The pages on both sides are the same. This is why DTP programs have the option of facing pages. When creating grids with large margins, don't be afraid to use page setup commands to give yourself large margins to work with, but remember that these may be non-printing areas.

Here the grid almost reads straight across the spine gutter. Experimentation with the spaces at the top and bottom of pages compared to the spaces at the sides shows that a wide variety of grids are available. DTP systems will allow you to see immediately which layout best suits the text and image content of the job.

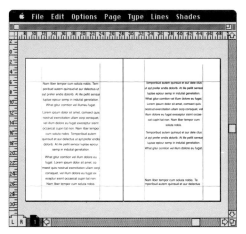

This grid has two centered columns of centered type. It would be perfectly symmetrical apart from the smaller aside at the bottom right, which has been used to break the grid and create a point of interest. This is hard to see in isolation, but if this were an unusual page in 20 continuous pages using the centered design, it would work well.

This grid incorporates a space for photographs that very much belong with the text. The boxes have been left deliberately wide so a large size of type will read comfortably.

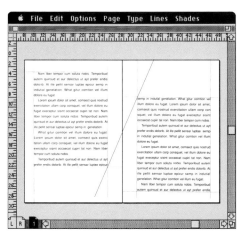

This grid is symmetrical but in an unusual way. The differentiation between left and right pages is indicated by a vertical displacement.
Such a layout might include small images to balance the white spaces.

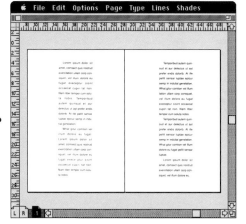

In this format the text is very narrow. This will allow large margins for illustrations or pictures at the side. This would obviously be suitable for a manual, for example.

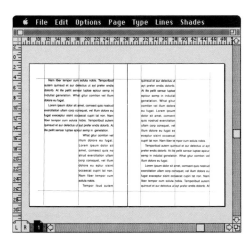

Here, a lot of work went into creating an interesting master spread with holes in the block of text, designed for inserting images. Although complicated to set up at first, this design would be fairly easy to use, as the size of the holes can be varied depending on how much text needs to be accommodated.

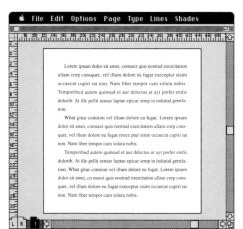

This is a square format – a very satisfying shape for layout. A classical centered single column with classical proportioned margins always works well.

Organizing Your Page/2

Grids are an essential layout tool in the design of books, magazines, newspapers, company reports, presentational documents – indeed most printed graphic media. A series of advertisements will use a similar or even identical grid design, so that each single ad will be recognized as belonging to the series, even if each will only ever be seen separately. Similarly, a small range of personal stationery – or the entire graphic output of a large corporation – can be unified by means of a grid.

With two or more columns of text to consider, the layout grid becomes more complex. Apart from specifying the page margins, we also have to consider the space between columns (the gutter), and the horizontal components of the grid that will determine the placing of new sections of text.

Ideally, the grid should define the relative positions of all the graphic elements that appear on the page. But designers do not feel that they are unduly restricted by this and break the grid design where they feel it necessary, in order to add variety and emphasis to their design.

Remember that the grid design is derived from a careful analysis of the graphic problem – in terms of logical, technical, audience, and budgetary constraints – as well as from the actual prototype layout designs expressed as thumbnails and roughs.

This is the most basic of all multiple-column grids, the justified two-column grid. This standard example has normal margins and looks extremely plain. This design would not really be suitable for any but the most basic document.

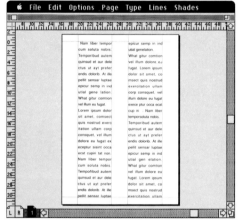

On this page, a two-column grid was used. In an A4 publication you may find that the width of half a page gives a line length for normal text type (9 point or 10 point) that is a little too long for the eye to comfortably follow. The ways around this are either to bring in your margins or to use a large central gutter.

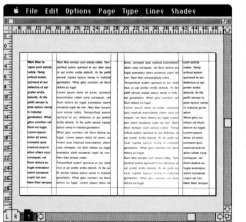

Here we see a totally symmetrical grid, with two different column widths for related elements of information. Fine in theory, but two different stories rarely run concurrently in length, so two relevant pieces of information might be on different pages.

CHECK**LIST**

- Page layout is not just a visual problem; it must reinforce the communication of content.

- Consider page size and format in terms of function and purpose.

- Successful grids will allow the designer considerable freedom in the layout of each individual page.

- Experiment with the size of the column gutters (space between columns).

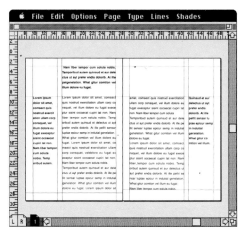

This is a more realistic version of one of the parallel grids on this page, where horizontal guides have also been used to impose consistency on the positioning of type.

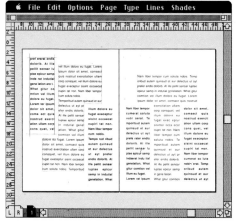

Here the element that makes the grid is area, rather than position. This means that equal areas are arranged in different ways on the pages. The designs are composed of three basic units: one large text box and two long, thin text boxes. By arranging the elements differently the pages all look interestingly varied while still maintaining a visual consistency.

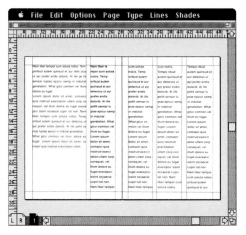

Grids do not have to be the same on left-hand and righthand pages. The sample grid here, which would be uniform for the entire publication, uses the leftmost column for an overview or introduction and the other four columns for more detailed nitty gritty.

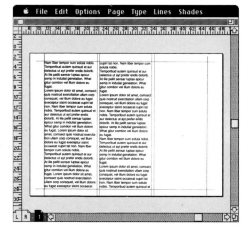

Something that shouldn't be forgotten when organizing your page is the orientation of the page. Producing in a landscape format can be a very effective way of getting noticed. However you will have to pay great attention to the sequence in which text should be read, especially if your page folds in the center of a column.

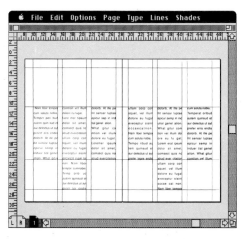

This simple three-column grid is made distinctive by the use of important horizontal guides. Too often grids are designed just using column guides. The spaces at the top and bottom allow for pictures and captions to be dropped in.

Organizing Your Page/3

Certain types of publications – especially magazines and newsletters – can have different styles of layout to reflect the content of different editorial sections. To cope with this intended variety of layout within their pages the designer produces a grid that can be used in several different ways – a mixed grid.

A mixed grid can simply offer a different grid for each facing page – say a two-column grid on the righthand (recto) page, and a three-column grid for the lefthand (verso) page. Or a grid can be devised that will allow the designer to use two, three, four (or more) columns on each page, as the content – or his intuition – dictates. Complex mixed grids like this have to be very carefully designed so that the overall style of the whole publication remains intact, while at the same time allows the designer extra layout options.

In newspapers, for example, a mixed grid might offer eight narrow columns for its news pages, where the information density is high, and six wider columns for its editorial and features sections, where longer articles demand that the text be readable. Often newspapers will use justified text for news, with ranged-left text for features. So the grid also depends on the overall house style developed for the particular publication.

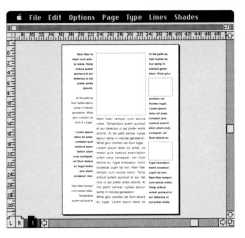

This is actually a four-column grid, not three; the central text takes up two of the four columns. Notice also the use of ranging specific to a column. The left column ranges right and the right column ranges left. Together with the central justified column, an outward dynamism is achieved.

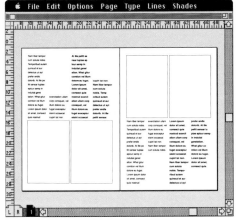

This design is about relating text to pictures. A grid of four columns was used. The first column of each two-column caption is aligned with the top or bottom margin. The second column of each caption is then left to hang. Aligning blocks by their bottoms rather than their tops is a tricky process.

This is a vertically centered layout. Ranging the text underneath the pictures is easy, but the blocks on the upper half of the page had to be carefully set to force the endings to align horizontally.

This is an example of a mixed grid. The top half of the spread is set across two columns, while the lower half is on three. The basic design for such a layout that allows these combinations is a six-column grid. The difference in measure serves to distinguish items from one another.

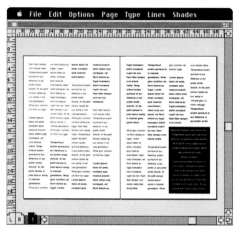

This is a straight four-column grid. The narrow measure on these columns makes the text feel pacy, hence the style is suitable for a newsletter or briefing section but not for an in-depth feature. Here, alternating stories have been set in bold and roman to make it clear where stories begin and end, and a separate piece has been set across two columns to break up the page.

This demonstrates use of a dummy column to give some space on the page. It is most suitable for a brochure. At the same time as making the page look more attractive, this layout technique allows you to allocate a consistent place on every page to place extra information, such as addresses, quotations, marginal notes, or captions as in this book.

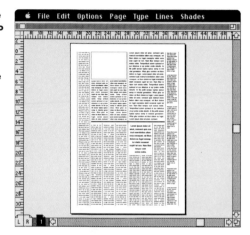

This eight-column grid would only be suitable for a large format or tabloid publication. However the multiple columns allow for a good deal of variety, combining single, double or triple measures, all of which are legible.

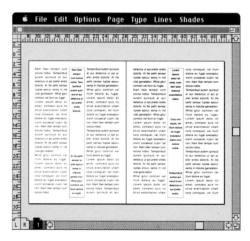

This is an interesting way of combining extra information. We have here the same components as the dummy column grid previously illustrated, but centering the extra information spreads the body text and breaks up the grayness of the text blocks.

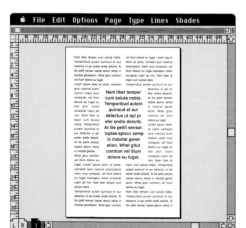

This two-column grid comfortably accommodates an excerpt, which acts as an easy starter to pull the reader in. This would work well for a booklet where parallel information needs to be inserted within blocks of text.

High-Quality Typesetting

Because DTP systems can make the designer responsible for both sub-editing and typesetting, it is important that you develop a system that will allow for adequate copy checking and error correction. It's also important to learn to pay attention to every small detail of the typesetting process.

For example, setting justified text over short measures can lead to ugly and distracting rivers of white space. These can sometimes be rectified by adjusting the word spacing so that the empty space on one line does not occur vertically over the empty space in the line below. Sometimes this can be done by taking a short word (a, an, of, if, the, etc) up on to the line above, but sometimes it will involve adding space in different places, editing the text, or forcing a word break by inserting your own hyphenation or adding extra words.

It is important to develop your own set of house rules – rules that govern all matters of typographical style for a particular publication. House rules should define when and where you use different faces and typeface variants and how measure, leading, word spacing, indention, paragraph spacing, headings, sub-headings and captions are to be set and used within the page layout. These rules will help you to achieve a consistency in style throughout a DTP job.

◆ CHECK**LIST**

- Leading is measured from baseline to baseline and includes the point size of the type.

- Use em dashes instead of ordinary hyphens for sentence breaks and en dashes between numbers.

- Use properly sexed quotation marks, not the vertical marks available in word processor packages.

- Don't use the underline option.

- Text set justified to a short measure is prone to unsightly rivers of white space.

- Avoid widows.

- Text set solid (with no leading) can cause interference between ascenders and descenders.

- Develop your own house rules for the use of different fonts, variants, measures, leading, etc, to insure consistency throughout a particular job.

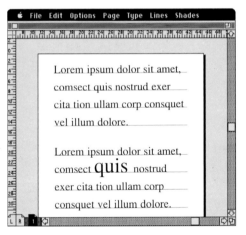

The word processor measures leading from the top of the characters in one line to the top of the characters in the line below. When setting one word of the line in larger type, the leading will measured from the tops of the taller characters and the line below will be squashed up. It will be impossible to align columns, so use the typesetting leading mode instead.

True typesetting leading is measured from one baseline to the next so that lines of text will align correctly across columns.

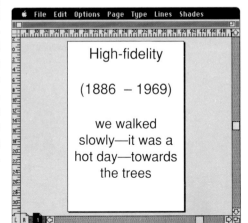

High-fidelity

(1886 – 1969)

we walked slowly—it was a hot day—towards the trees

To achieve professional typesetting, it is important to use correct punctuation characters. "High-fidelity" uses a standard hyphen. However between numbers you should use an "en" dash, often achieved by typing the hyphen key with "alt" or "option" buttons. The third example shows an "em" rule, used to break two parts of a sentence.

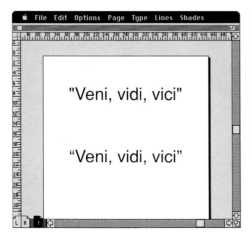

It is not a good idea to use straight up and down quotes as in the top example. Instead you should substitute properly sexed quotes, which will be directly available with most professionally produced type fonts, seen here in bottom example.

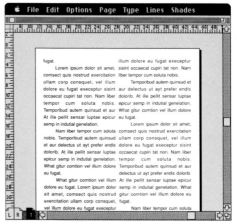

"Widows" are another typesetter's gremlin. A widow is the last word or line on its own at the end of a paragraph, at the top of a column or on a new page as on the top left here. These are conventionally avoided by editing. You can change the design instead, but you should avoid changing leading or anything that might detract from the consistency of the design.

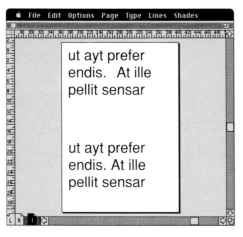

A convention taught to typists is to put two spaces after periods (as in the top example). This is not true for typesetting, where the finer width settings allow for a single space after punctuation. You should also watch out for the insertion of spaces before punctuation . (like that).

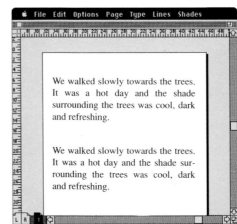

You may find that your system over-spaces words and letters in order to justify a line (see second line of top example). This looks ugly and you should consider hyphenating the first word of the next line (see second line of bottom example).

One of the things good typesetters strive to avoid is "rivers" in text. When word spaces occur next to each other on consecutive lines, the reader's eye can be distracted into following the white spaces that are created. This example has a vertical river almost in the center of the page that has been deliberately exaggerated to draw your attention to it.

Introducing Typefaces

The main classification of typefaces is determined by whether or not the letter forms end in a finishing stroke, or serif. Throughout the long history of printing, serif faces have been used for text settings, mainly because the horizontal motion of the eye scanning along lines of text is reinforced by the horizontal serifs. Serifs also modulate the spaces between letters, giving serif text a softer, more delicate appearance that is more suitable for continuous reading.

Faces that have no serif endings are called sans serifs. Most designers would recommend extra leading for long texts set in sans serif, as the increased line spacing reinforces the horizontal, again helping the eye scan along the lines of text. Sans serifs are much more successful for shorter texts and texts not intended for continuous reading, such as catalogues and timetables.

The two styles of typeface have very different connotations. Serif faces refer back to classical times and carry an aura of authority and formality, whereas sans serifs present a clean, modern and functional aspect. Because they are subliminal and therefore not consciously noticed by the average reader, these connotations can have a powerful effect in establishing the context in which the text is to be read. The designer must consider the text content and choose a face that will establish a suitable context for it.

Two sans serif faces: above, the informative Helvetica, currently the most popular typeface in the world, and below, geometric Futura, a very attractive font that needs a lot of leading to be legible. Futura is used here in the condensed medium bold version – look at how much more text you can accommodate in the same space!

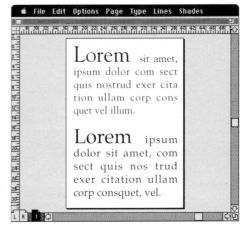

Two serif faces: above the overtly classical Goudy, with elegant long ascenders, and, below, the more recently designed (1950) Palatino. The difference in linespacing between the two is not caused by extra leading in the Goudy text but is a design feature of Goudy, allowing enough space for the long ascenders.

Slab serifs are square and chunky. Sometimes they are bracketed, where the point at which they join the rest of the character is rounded. They are good for solid no-nonsense information like catalogues and price lists.

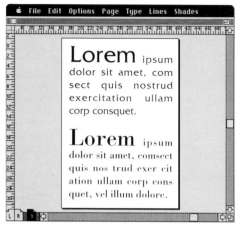

Wedge serifs are triangular serifs that have no soft bracketed joints to the rest of the character. Friz Quadrata is a very elegant serif face that approaches a wedge serif style. Note the characters where the strokes do not join up, giving the face a very calligraphic quality. The bottom face, Bodoni, is an example of a hairline serif – one with very thin, elongated serifs that add a strong horizontal influence to the text.

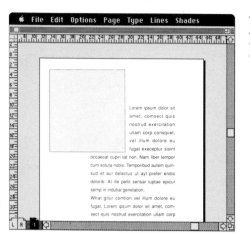

This modern asymmetrical layout would suit a sans serif font such as Helvetica.

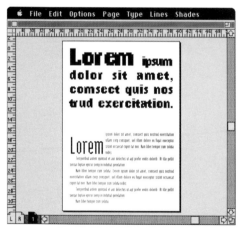

Another variety of type available to DTP users are bitmapped faces. This is type designed primarily for a computer display, composed of squares that are either black (on) or white (off). This style of lettering has a beauty all of its own, and some magazines use the limitations of low-resolution dot-matrix printers to make a design point.

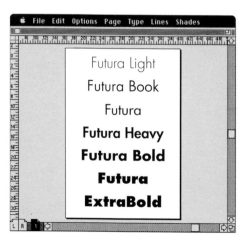

Aesthetic considerations are not the only things to influence your choice of type. Here we see exactly the same passage of text typeset in exactly the same size and leading but in two different fonts. On the left is Times-Roman, a highly legible and economic typeface. On the right is the same passage set in Futura, which takes up much more space.

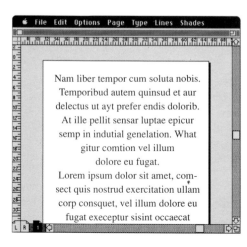

The typeface you choose must be suited to the content of the text and to the style of your layout. At the lowest common denominator level, serif is classical and sans serif is modern. Here a classically centered layout was produced using Times-Roman, the most common of all serif typefaces, usually supplied with DTP packages.

To add variety within a piece of text, many weights are available in each typeface. In DTP this group of different weights for the same typeface is called a type family. When more than two weights are available in the required font you will have to choose the typeface you want rather than just clicking bold.

Using Captions

Captions can have several functions within a page design. They are an editorial device for leading the reader from illustrations or photographs into the main body of the text. They enable the writer to allude to material not possible to include in the main text. They allow the designer to add color (in the sense of text tone) to a layout and to visually relate image and text blocks together, using the caption as a transition device.

Because they are physically separate from the main body text, captions should be treated in a contrasting typographic style, either by using a variant (bold, italic or condensed perhaps), a different point size, a different measure, or a different, but complementary typeface – or perhaps by a combination of these methods. In some cases, the distinction between the caption and a text lead-in can be purposely blurred, perhaps wrapping the caption around part of the image before carrying the eye down into the body text.

Alternatively, text set justified or ranged-left can be complemented by captions set ranged-right. This is a useful device, as it clearly separates text and captions in situations where there may be some confusion between the two, such as in a spread that features a large image and only a small amount of body text.

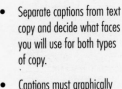

CHECK**LIST**

- Separate captions from text copy and decide what faces you will use for both types of copy.

- Captions must graphically relate to the images they describe. Decide how your captions will do this.

- Try using a dummy column for images and captions.

- How can you make captions stand out from the body text?

- Can captions be made to relate both to an image and to the relevant passage of body text?

- Try wrapping the caption text around part of the image area.

- Try including the caption within the image area.

- Try ranging the caption in a different and complementary way to the body text.

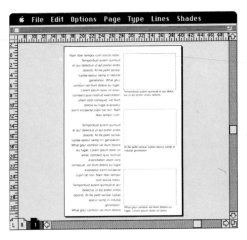

There is no confusion on this page as to which pictures the captions belong. This is achieved by making each caption very close to its relevant picture and far away from the next picture. The main text ranges right towards the pictures and the captions range left. This creates a center of gravity along an imaginary vertical central axis.

This is a Big Caption. Sounds obvious, but it is all too often taken for granted that captions should be smaller than body text. By indenting the photo into the caption the viewer immediately reads the caption, thus turning from browser to reader. If it is a well-written caption, the reader will be encouraged to read the body text.

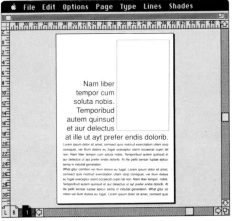

In this example full use has been made of a caption column. That is the outermost column on the page that has been reserved for caption text only. This organizes the page and allows the browser to merely read through the pictures and associated short text.

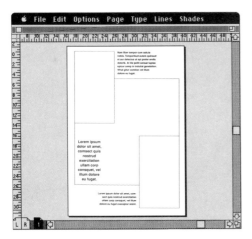

On complicated pages with more than one photo it is important to use visual signposts to indicate which caption belongs with which picture. Here the top and bottom photos have captions that range against them. The larger central photo has a larger caption whose type is centered. The final indicator is that the larger caption is within the larger photo.

This caption is distinguished from the body text by being leaded more than the body text. This makes the gray value of the caption more attractive and thus the first thing the viewer will read.

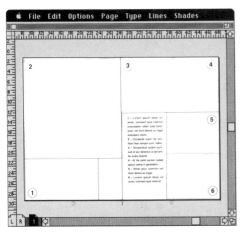

In this page from a catalogue it was impossible to have the captions immediately next to the text so the practice of numbering was used. The difficulty comes when deciding which picture should be number one!

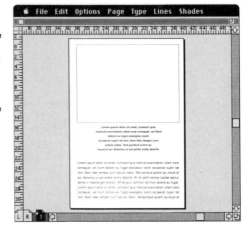

Here a long caption is centered under the picture. This and its position in the middle of the page make the caption important.

This photo-intensive page had a present style for the captions, specifying they must be ranged left. Thus a strict grid was imposed on the pictures and their captions to make it clear which belonged with which.

Introductions

B y introductions we mean those text devices that are used to lead the reader's eye into the beginning of the body text (as opposed to captions that may lead anywhere within the text). Introductions are used to engage the reader's interest at the beginning of a magazine feature or section of a book or report, although many of the devices illustrated in this section can also be used to enliven pages that would otherwise comprise just body text on its own.

Introductory text components like these take on something of the role of an illustration on the page, and they rely on the use of a typeface, point size and layout that is very different from, but complementary to, that used for the body text. Having the scale and function of an illustration, an introductory paragraph might be set in a particularly decorative display face. It should be carefully word spaced to enhance the surrounding white space.

Introductions set in large sizes can effectively fill a double spread, acting as a long headline, before reducing in size down to body text.

Different measures can also be used effectively, perhaps running the opening paragraph across two or three columns of a multi-column grid, or breaking the grid to form a single block indented into two text columns.

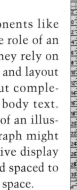

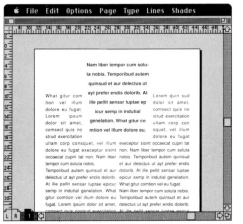

This is the simplest format of all for saying "here's where it starts" – the introductory paragraph is the same typeface, size and measure as the body text. The only thing that distinguishes it is position – where it is on the page (at the top) and what is next to it (nothing) it's that important.

This well-known format for introducing a new story involves setting the first paragraph across a wider measure than the rest of the text – a double column in fact – and emboldening it. Quick and effective, people know what they're getting, but it is very uninspiring.

This is a similar example to the above layout except it takes advantage of DTP runaround facilities. Due to the difficulty involved in achieving effects like this conventionally, this style of indenting the first paragraph is fairly unusual, although just as effective as the first example. However problems may arise over placement of headings.

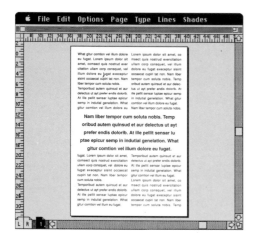

The first paragraph doesn't necessarily have to be at the top of the page. As long as it is set different from the body text, the viewer will know that this is the introductory paragraph and go to it first. Using conventions like a larger point size or bold type will help signpost the way.

This unusual read-in was easy to create using keyboard controls to step characters up and down in one-point increments. To conventionally typeset something like this would require a separate instruction string for each change. Creative use of the features of DTP packages can open doors to all kinds of new effects.

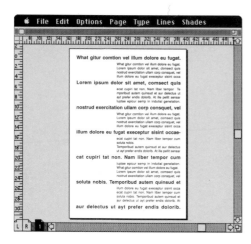

This introductory paragraph is unusually spaced out, but because it is sufficiently distinguished from the rest of the text and also intrudes into the dummy column, it still reads well. This style may be more appropriate to an ad or display setting.

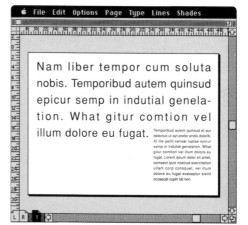

This is what's called a full page read-in – blurring the borders between introduction and heading. Of course to do this it helps to have a very strong first line of copy. The introduction is read straight across and into the body text.

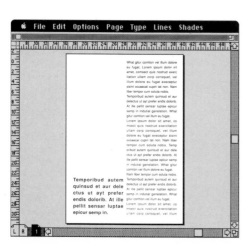

On this page the introduction is the first thing discovered by the eye as it travels horizontally, but the last thing discovered vertically. However the type's larger point size indicates that it should be read first.

Text Devices/ Drop Capitals

The manuscript calligraphers of medieval Europe are the source of much modern graphic design. Perhaps the most noticeable device we have inherited from them is that of the enlarged initial capital letter. Today this can be used in the same way as the scribes used illuminated capitals – to draw the reader's eye to the beginning of chapters and section headings, and to add contrast to the main body of text. Because they form a very noticeable part of the page, they must be carefully considered as to how they link into the body text and how they create space between themselves and the text.

Probably the most usual way they are used is as drop caps – initial capital letters that are indented into the body text. The drop cap should span an exact number of text lines and align exactly, baseline to baseline, with the lower line of text. Optical rather than true alignment should be used, giving due consideration to the shape of the initial capital and to how it fits with the body text. Rigid true alignment can give the optical effect of not being aligned properly; adjustment has to be made so that it looks right.

Like all emphasis in typography, large initial capitals should be used sparingly; overuse can mar both their optical function and their decorative effect.

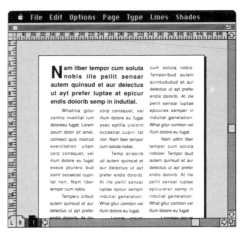

This shows four stages of development of a drop cap. First a plain three-line drop cap. Next it was decided to change it to a drop two lines/raise one cap. The third example is a plain raised cap, obtained by increasing the character's point size. Then the raised cap was set in a different typeface.

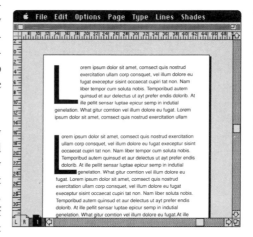

This example shows the universally useful drop capital. Here the drop cap indents into the first paragraph, which itself indents into two of the three columns of text. The point size of the three elements also steps down logically.

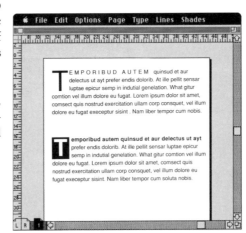

These two illustrations show the difference between normal and runaround drop caps. Some programs will let you run type around other type from within the program. Otherwise you may need to prepare the capital letters you will require in a graphics program and import them.

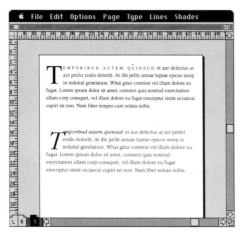

The drop cap takes many forms. Top: the first two words have been capitalized and letterspaced. Second: a "wobbed" drop cap. The first line of type has also been set in bold. Care has been taken to evenly outset the first three lines from the edge of the black box.

In a publication, drop caps are likely to be used for visual effect rather than at points dictated by the text. Read some magazines – the drop cap positions often have no sense of the story!

The first line here has been set with spaced-out small capitals, a traditional combination with drop caps. Italic drop caps don't work too well.

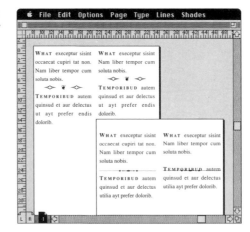

Using Zapf Dingbats instead of imported, separate graphics means that if text is edited the Dingbats will reflow with the text, whereas the graphic will remain in its original position and obscure the repositioned text.

A page where every paragraph uses drop caps might be considered overdoing it. However, using a large three-line drop cap at the top of the page followed by simpler two-liners helps give the page some variety.

Numbers are extremely graphic. Often a page has been rescued by use of some judicious numbering applied at the last stage by the designer. Here some numerals from the Zapf Dingbats font have been used to number the paragraphs.

Text Devices/ Pull Quotes

Apart from the use of initial capitals, there is a range of other devices that may be used, either functionally or decoratively, on a text page. Many of these devices are also inspired by manuscript layout. Medieval scribes would often leave large margins around the text blocks in order to accommodate marginal notes. Marginalia had the effect of breaking up the hard rectilinear space of the body text, adding emphasis and interest to the page. We can achieve this same effect by means of establishing dummy columns especially for the purpose of displaying pull quotes (excerpts from the body text that are pulled out of context and used rather in the same way that captions are, to attract the reader to an especially interesting point).

Pull quotes can be displayed in a variety of different ways, indenting the quote into body text at the side, top, bottom or center of the text columns. Having a display function on the page, the pull quotes can be set in a different typeface, as well as in a different point size to the body text.

Try setting the pull quote in type reversed out of a panel of black, or using extra large quotation marks, or setting the quote on a curved baseline. Whatever technique you use, make sure that it is contextually relevant.

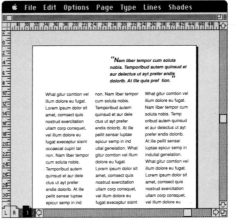

This is a pull quote, a quote pulled from the main text. Placed in the "hot-spot" at the top right of a right-hand page, it's the first thing a viewer sees on turning the page. They have to read the quote, and if it's enticing enough they'll read the rest of the text.

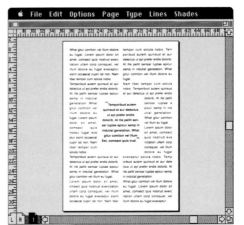

This is the conventional place to position a pull quote: within the story from which it came, centered neatly, with type running around. For the best effect the quote needs to be centered on the gutter between two columns.

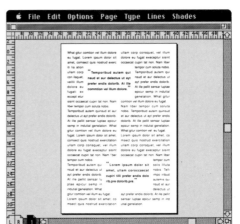

Different displacement around the central gutter allows two quotes to be included without looking repetitive. Swinging the quotes around the central page axis gives the page a visual dynamic.

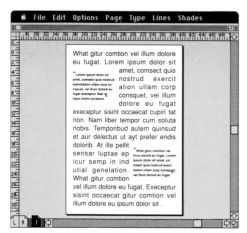

This is a similar arrangement to the previous illustration but shows the quotes indented into the side edges of the body text. Because the type here goes over quite a long measure (a full A4 page width) the point size was increased to make it readable. The quotes stand out despite their being smaller in size, because they have a darker tonal quality than the main text.

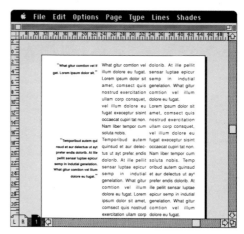

Full use has been made of a dummy column to pull out relevant quotes and place them next to where they occur in the copy. The disadvantage with this placement is that it doesn't cause the reader to scan the whole story to place the quote that caught his or her interest.

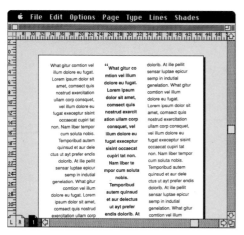

This neatly centered quote creates a large gutter between the two columns of text, allowing them a shorter, more readable measure. It's a useful device on a two-column grid where small type needs to be used.

Reversing out pull quotes, or "wobbing" them, is an effective way of distinguishing them from the rest of the text. Here a quote has been placed together with a portrait. Photos always liven up a page, and a pull-quote accompanied by even a snapshot session out-take is a bonus.

Bold sentences have been picked out within this text. This is a natural way of breaking up interviews with questions in bold and answers plain. The questions are usually in the minority compared to celebrities' windy answers! A whole page of bold type is difficult to read and needs more space, necessitating a smaller point size.

Rules and Boxes/1

Rules were originally simple strips of metal that could be inked and printed alongside type in a press. Over the centuries of printing, many ornate varieties of rules have been developed. Indeed, whole kits of printers' ornaments are available, including rules, corners, symbols and other embellishments, reflecting all the styles and fashions of type design.

Rules have four main functions. They can be used to: decorate and enhance information, such as a title; separate items of information; emphasize information; and lead the reader's eye from one part of the page to another. Fine hairline rules can be used to indicate the reference points for the labels to a diagram or bar chart, or to label a schematic map or drawing. Both rules and boxes formed from two horizontal and two vertical rules are used in slightly different ways to separate items on the page, to enhance a title block, and to emphasize points.

Because of the strong stylistic statements embodied in their decoration, the more decorative rules have to be considered in the same way as illustrations – that is, their style should complement the style of the typographic treatment of the text. For example, heavy black rules would look inappropriate as decoration on a party invitation.

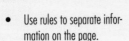

CHECK**LIST**

- Use rules to separate information on the page.

- Use rules to emphasize information.

- Rules can be used to guide the reader's eye across and down the page or spread.

- Make sure that the style of decorative rules fits the style of the whole page layout and the content of the text.

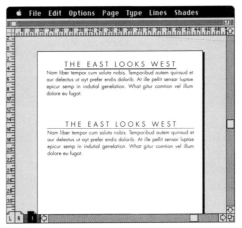

The top example here shows two beginners' common mistakes. The rule is too close to the type beneath it and too heavy for the typeface. The second example has the rule stretched across the width of the column, which is a more natural endpoint for the rule.

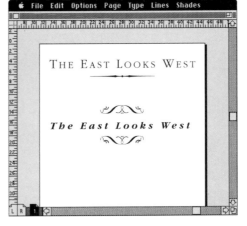

These fancy rules are all imported from graphics programs, which makes them difficult to use. The second example here shows some of the more decorative classical embellishments now available as clip-art.

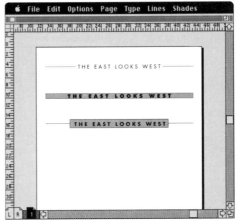

As well as placing the rule above and below the heading, it can be placed along a middle line. To do this properly the rule should be split in the center, which is usually quicker to do with another centered white-filled box than by drawing two separate halves of the rule.

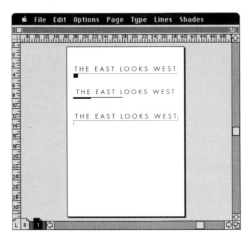

These modern rules are more suited to DTP production than the ornate classical rules; they are all combinations of horizontal and vertical lines. You should use "snap-to guides"— commands to make sure the rules don't overlap.

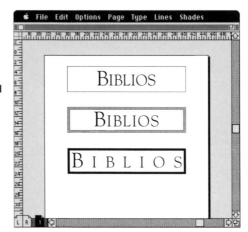

Experiment with the different frames available on your DTP system to understand what kind of image they project when printed.

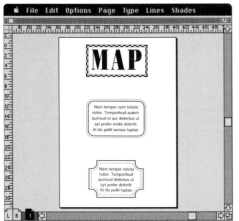

Some programs let you create custom frames, like XPress's Frame Editor, which was used for the top frame here. You may want to use a graphics program to draw a few special panels, but make sure that rounded corners are identical or the box will look distorted.

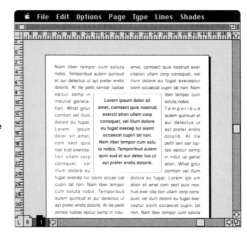

This pull quote has been separated from the rest of the story by a thin rule. This makes the quote self–contained, and thus more attractive to the browser.

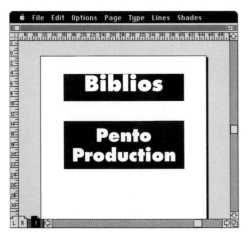

If placing text within a panel, take care that the same distance is left on all sides and between lines within the heading. This was not done on the top heading here as it was on the second.

Rules and Boxes/2

When using rules composed of thick and thin strokes ("Oxford" or "Scotch" rules) you should combine them in opposite pairs.

Plain rules, especially those of 2 points width and above, have been used as bold graphic devices by many graphic designers who had a dominant influence on modern typography. Plain rules were used, as they were considered to be more functional than decorative, and as they were often the only non-letter component of the design, they were used in a range of thicknesses.

Today, however, we can experiment with a much broader range of rules, with styles derived from many historical and geographical locations. Many books of type specimens and rules are available and are useful for reference if you wish to design your own rules or borders.

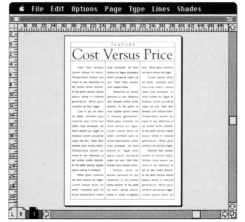

Ruling in the whole page (by creating page boxes) is a good way to make a layout appear extremely organized, as it makes the grid visible. This type of layout is common in news publications, as the rules allow for a variety of different text items.

Generally, rules and boxes should conform to the original grid layout, and they must adhere to an established set of your own house rules – always using the same type of box for quotes, another type for information, etc, so that the reader can identify a logical plan in your presentation of information. Rules and boxes can be used together to create schematic diagrams, bar charts and flow charts, and the precision possible in DTP makes the production of this sort of line artwork far quicker and more effective than traditional equivalents.

Inter-column (gutter) rules improve legibility of densely set type. Where there is insufficient room for proper gutters, they stop the eye from roaming across two columns. A 1-pica (about 4.2 mm) gap is normal. Be careful to align the bottom of the rule with the baseline of the bottom line of type.

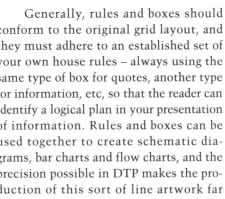

◆ CHECK**LIST**

- Full-page boxes can give a sense of unity to pages comprising several different bits of information.

- Newsletter layouts may need column gutter rules to separate different items.

- Use different weights of rule on the same page but use them consistently: thick rules for separating text items, thin rules for guiding the reader's eye.

- Boxes and tinted panels can be used to isolate items like captions, pull quotes, introductions, etc, from the main text.

Using different weights of rules on the horizontal and vertical axes tells the reader which line to follow to find the rest of the story. Different types of rules can also be used to indicate "different" things – ie, "different" stories or "different" sections.

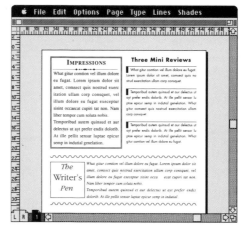

This design uses various types of rule to signify different things – boxing off one article and separating a regular column with a cus-tom-drawn wavy line.

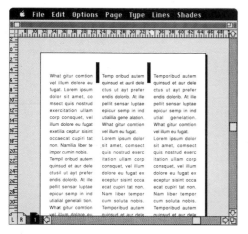

A modern derivative of column rules is the column slab, a simple separating device that creates a strong enough vertical element to separate columns on a page.

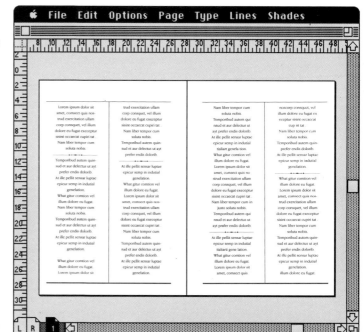

Rules can be used to hold stories together; here a thick rule bleeds across the center of the page and tells the reader to follow across the spine of the publication. It also breaks the spread into two stories.

Rules can hold a design together. Here a small ornamental rule is used as a repeated motif, breaking up the grayness of all text pages and leading the eye from one piece of text to another, almost like a logo for the text.

Creating Headings

The effectiveness of a heading depends as much on its content as on the style in which it's treated, but the scale, or relative size, of the heading ensures its prominence on the page. Effective visual tricks can be played with scale, the most powerful being the simple devices of inversion and juxtaposition. For example you can treat an ampersand (&) in a heading as a major decorative device by grossly enlarging it, so that its subservient role becomes dominant in juxtaposition to the rest of the heading. Lowercase letters can be set at enormously large point sizes, in contrast with small capitals; punctuation marks and small graphic symbols can be distorted in scale, etc.

Of course, all these treatments depend on their relevant application to the text and to the intended style and treatment of the publication. Remember that graphic design is the careful balance resulting from a logical analysis of the content of the text and a consideration of the aesthetics of the page. A bad headline may be improved visually by a stylish graphic treatment, but this will not necessarily enhance the communication of the author's message.

Headings are akin to illustrations in the way that they can express the content of the text and the style in which it has been written.

CHECK**LIST**

- Consider the visual shapes made by headings.

- Establish a coherent and consistent system for headings.

- Use rules to help integrate headings and text.

- Reverse out headings to create a strong visual link with the text columns and paper edges.

- Use a different, complementary typeface for headings.

- Try inventing your own type for headings.

Taller condensed characters on the bottom example here are actually more legible than the extended ones on the top example due to the angle people actually view the page from.

Headings can be enhanced by a variety of techniques. In these examples a word has been reversed out, weights of the same typeface have been mixed together, Zapf Dingbats have been used.

Opera is the most important word, so to make the two lines justify the type size was increased.

In order to justify the two lines in this example, it was decided to add letterspacing and keep the sizes constant.

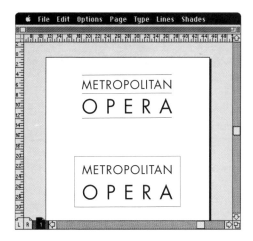

To augment the importance of a heading on a page you may choose to add rules.

Positioning the second line of this heading at an angle adds a spontanelty that livens up the layout.

You may have a whole page to fit a heading into. Here the use of graphic elements livens up the page. If you do a heading like this in a graphics program you can import it and repeat it at different scales as a logo for a particular article.

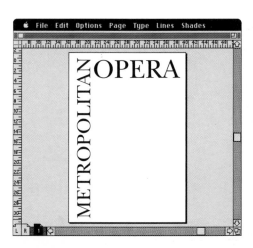

If there's an extremely long word (or words) in a heading you may find it useful to run it up the side of a page. The type should read along the outside edge of a page, and its baseline should face into the article.

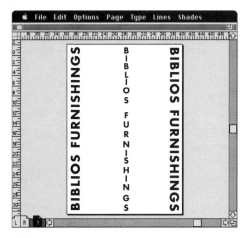

Experiment with the difference in legibility of reading vertical type.

Putting Headings With Text/1

Designers work very systematically. They develop a grid to establish a system of page layout, and they use house rules (or style sheets) to establish a system for dealing with typographic treatment. When we consider headings, subheadings, and text, it is obvious that there is a logical hierarchy of importance in their relationship, and it is the typographer's job to reflect this hierarchy visually – both in layout and in the choice of typefaces, sizes and variants. The importance of house rules is to establish a system for dealing with this hierarchy, so that the relative importance of headings, subheadings, etc, is reflected coherently throughout the publication. If rules or other graphic symbols are to be used to emphasize points within the text, then the grid must indicate a guide upon which they can be aligned.

The house rules on headings should determine the typeface, size, variant, and/or treatment (reversed-out, tinted panel, etc) for each level within the hierarchy of importance, while the grid should help establish the relative position for each level within the page layout. The important point here is consistency. Each publication – or each separate section within a publication – should be treated consistently regarding headings and subheadings. Consistency allows the reader to correctly interpret the hierarchy of information within each section and to differentiate between sections.

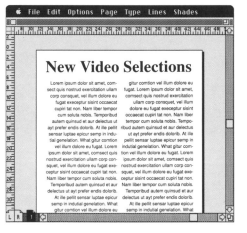

Decked, or multi-line headings were traditional in early newspaper design, where type was set in very narrow columns to accommodate the small point size of body type (often 7 or 8 point).

This typical layout runs the heading across two columns of type. However to make the design more interesting, the text was ranged-right.

By drawing rules across the page the main text is broken up. The headings are hung below the line (rather than the more conventional position above the line), so that the headings are on the same side of the line as their associated text.

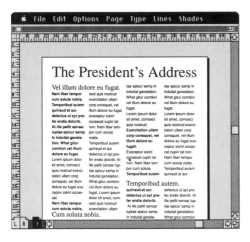

In this design, the importance of the heading is indicated by two factors: the size of type and the measure across which the type is set. Thus main headings are big, across four columns, and smaller headings run across two columns.

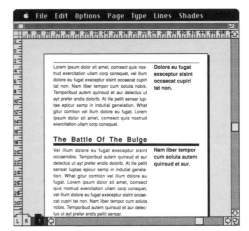

The main heading on this page created a problem because it came halfway down the page. It was drawn out by using a much heavier rule and a different placement of type relative to that rule.

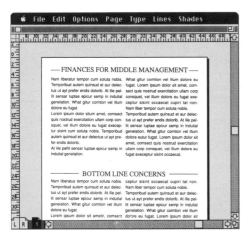

The type was justified in two columns. Rules were added to each side of the centered headings to bring them to full measure. In this way both headings have equal weight.

This layout marks the importance of headings by their measure – wider than the text. Such a layout is dependent upon the amount of space available.

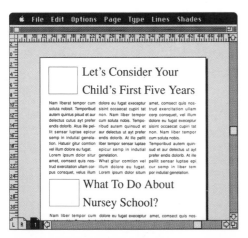

Each heading here is accompanied by an image that illustrates in brief what is covered in the paragraph following.

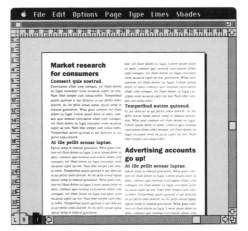

Another way of distinguishing levels of headings is choice of font. Different typefaces have inherent different relative to their weight.

Putting Headings with Text/2

Of course, titles, or main headings, that only appear once in a publication do not have to conform to house rules, and it is in the treatment of main headings that the typographic designer has the most freedom. Bear in mind the points we have stressed in earlier sections about the shape that a heading makes against the surrounding white space, and the positioning of text elements so that they relate to each other and to the shape and proportion of the page.

The main principle governing titles is that they should reflect the tone and content of the text that they introduce. You can do this typographically, by using an italic treatment to emphasize the word speed, for example, or graphically, by adding thin rules as speed lines, or by positioning – running the title off the edge of the paper, as though the heading is speeding away. The variations in treatment are infinite, but headings will not work effectively unless their graphic treatment is informed by a good idea – an idea that is related to their content.

Good ideas may call for special typographic treatments – distorting type or wrapping it around graphic shapes, for example. The power of the most sophisticated PostScript graphics software is approaching that enjoyed by professional designers using expensive photosetting facilities.

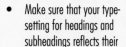

CHECK**LIST**

- Make sure that your typesetting for headings and subheadings reflects their position in the hierarchy of importance.

- Remember that subheadings break body copy into easily readable sections.

- Treat headings as though they were illustrations to the text – they must be stylistically and thematically relevant to the text content.

- Headings don't have to be at the top of the page!

To disguise the point where this heading crossed the central gutter of the spread the ampersand was enlarged in size. An extra gap was also put between "at" and "every."

This layout works well because the words are all of equal length. Also the type size is large enough to carry legibility across the split in the middle of the page.

This asymmetrical layout still allows the heading to be read as a separate item because it is set in a different font from the body text. The larger word binds the lead-in paragraph to the story.

In this heading, one meaningful word was picked out and made almost into an illustration. By having one word extremely large, the heading demands attention.

Some page layout programs offer you advanced features such as putting type in tints. This allows you to overlap body copy with headings, or reverse one tint of type out of another tint of background.

This heading contains two elements: the words and the number. The elements are treated separately, but by surrounding one with the other the eye is led through in the correct order.

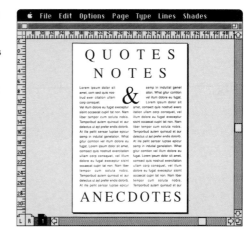

All of the heading doesn't have to be at the head of the page. By using a sufficiently bold typeface and large size the eye still reads this heading first.

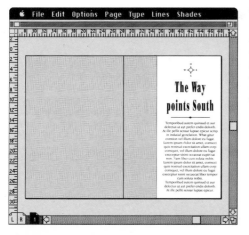

This basic layout reads coherently in sequence from left to right, top to bottom: photo, heading, text. All elements are unobtrusively complementary.

This balanced, classically centered layout is complemented by using small capitals for the heading, followed by roman letters for the subheading.

Matching the Face to the Job

CHECKLIST

- Study the typefaces in your system. What stylistic connotations do they have? Make a list of all the references they have for you.

- Sometimes the name of a typeface can be a clue as to how it should be used.

- Serif faces are generally more traditional in feel; sans serif faces are more modern.

- Typewriter faces are more folksy, script faces very romantic, bold faces are very forceful and masculine.

- Some typefaces are stylistically linked to the period in which they were designed.

- Display type should be illustrative of the theme or the style of the text.

- Use a drawing package to invent your own illustrative lettering.

- Use a dictionary or thesaurus for ideas on how to present a word or phrase.

- Scan in a roughly drawn title and edit it as a bitmap.

Typefaces have characters that are as individual as people. In one sense typefaces are abstract symbols, merely existing as vehicles for the sounds we make when we speak. In another sense, and often this is a sixth sense that is not consciously noticed by the average reader, each typeface carries another message – one of style.

The style of typefaces can be very subtle. We've already mentioned the effect that serif faces, like Times Roman, can have – a quiet authority, a dignity, an assuredness, based on its origins in classical culture. Conversely, sans serifs can send the message of modernity. With display faces, the range and variety of styles is much more extensive, allowing the designer far greater precision in reinforcing the author's message – the one that is embodied in the content of the text.

Choosing type for display purposes is rather like choosing a style of illustration to match the content of the illustration. Designers describe this as matching form with function. This section illustrates many of the possibilities. In each case we've chosen what seemed to us the obvious face to use. This ability to choose the right face grows out of experience in looking at and experimenting with an enormous variety of type.

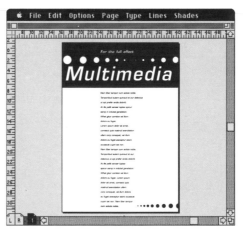

For this fast-moving media company, a modern face, Eurostile (aka Microgramma), was used. Its squared-off edges and extended look were matched with a shrinking dot, which was created with Adobe Illustrator's "in-betweening" function.

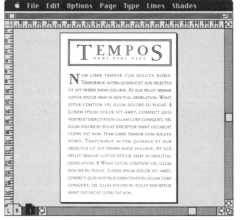

Tempos wanted a mock-Roman image so this inline typeface was specially created for them on the computer. However, custom fonts usually cause problems when printing in large areas, and this combined with the heading font's fussiness made Goudy Small Capitals the choice for accompanying material (note the extra leading for the text set in small caps).

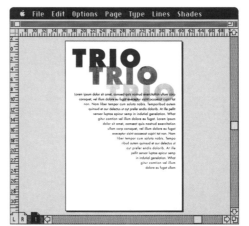

The manufacturer's name, Trio, gave the idea for this repeating layout which was done directly in the page layout program. Thus a font with a large surface area had to be chosen so that the tint would not be lost: Futura Extra-bold was chosen.

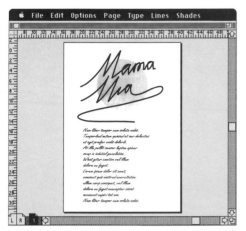

This Italian Pasta Bar wanted a handwritten logo, which was done quickly on the computer. Using computer drawing programs you can rough out some lines, then go in and edit the curves. Handwriting all the type was avoided by using Freestyle Script but intercharacter spacing had to be taken out to get the letters to join up.

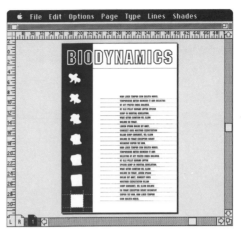

Biodynamics, manufacturers of prosthetic devices, wanted a computerized and machined feel. Thus Machine was used. The outlining effect was achieved in a graphics program. However this font has no lowercase so is not suitable for long copy.

This piece of promotional material for a classical concert demanded the most formal of approaches. Palace Script was used because it is legible for small blocks of copy such as this. However the generalization that upper- and lowercase is more legible than all capitals is very true with this font.

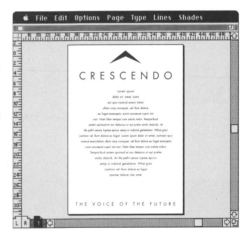

Crescendo sell extremely upmarket music gear, so they liked the refined geometric type of Futura. Choosing the lightest weight for the heading and adding lots of spacing creates a spacious feel, but it demands good quality printing!

Lunar Developments wanted to go all the way with a computer feel. Bit-map type was used, which allowed all their correspondence to be output on low-cost dot-matrix printers with no loss in quality. To make a font bit-map simply, remove the "printer" half of the font from the computer's system directory.

Homemade wanted a real cottage industry look, so Stencil was used for the logo. It looks like it has been cut out of a card and sprayed on. After paying for an expensive laserprinter, the letters looked too fancy, too typeset to be friendly. So they were set in Courier, a typewriter font.

Headers, Folios and Footers

◆ CHECK**LIST**

- Decide if you need a running head for the whole document or just to head different sections.

- Running heads are the type that appears at the top of every page.

- The folio is the individual page number. Pagination is the numbering of all the pages consecutively.

- Remember that there are different styles for page numbering: numeric, roman, decimal, alphanumeric, etc.

- Consider the fore-edge (outer) margin for page numbers.

- Try graphic devices instead of page numbers for short documents.

- How does the typeface for your page numbers contrast with the main text and with other type components on the page?

- Try using circles and square panels to reverse out page numbers.

The terms headers and footers derive from the parts of a page on which they appear. The head (or top) margin of a page of a book is traditionally used to carry a running head – the title of the book or magazine, or the chapter or section title, or both – that appears on every page. This information can also be carried in the foot, or bottom, margin. Footnotes, and other references out of the main body text also appear at the foot of the page.

Head and foot margins can also be used to carry the folio, or page number. (The term folio goes back over 2,000 years to when both sides of prepared animal skins were used as a surface for writing. These skins were folded (thus folio) once, to give a manageable size. The name is now used to denote a sheet of paper of any basic size that is folded once, and also the page number given to each page.) Folios can also be positioned along the fore-edge (the side of a page opposite the spine); in such cases the scale or style of type used should be distinct from the body text.

When you are choosing the style and position of the folio, keep in mind the entire pagination (the consecutive numbering of pages in a publication). The folio style must be one that will look good repeated on every (or almost every) page. And since the folio will be positioned in the same place throughout, that space must remain free for the folio.

A very neat, classical solution: the footer is set in capitals and a bullet separates it from the folio.

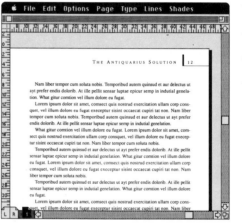

This and the following show two ways of enlivening a rather staid running head in capitals. Here a modern-looking rule encloses the folio.

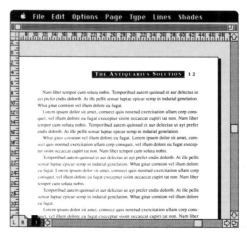

Here the running head is white out of black, which makes it easy to use as a device when searching for a particular item.

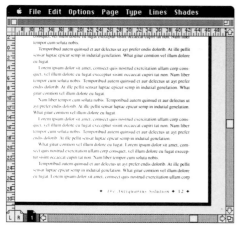

Very plain text can take a lively footer and still look serious. Three Dingbats enclose the footer and separate the words from the folio. Set in italics, the footer looks lightweight and the Dingbats help to steady it.

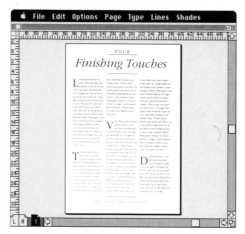

This classic-looking brochure uses numbers spelt out in full. While this works well for single-digit numbers, "one hundred and three" becomes cumbersome.

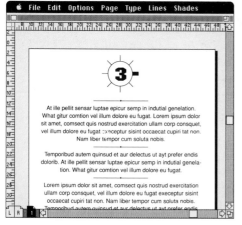

Within small publications there is no reason why a graphic device cannot be substituted for page numbers. This eight-spoked wheel was used as a rotating device for an eight-page brochure. Cryptic at first, but people are aided by their association with clockfaces.

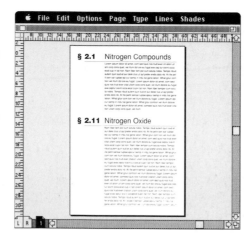

Because this booklet had more than one heading per page, each of which needed referencing, an indexing system involving decimals was used. This allows extra sections to be added later (2.1, followed by 2.11, 2.12). This system is often used for academic and scientific papers.

Old-fashioned Roman numerals have been used with a modern hairline rule here. By using a typeface with an exaggerated thick/thin serif the two components match.

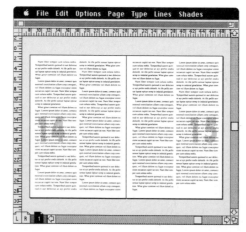

Some DTP packages have the ability to set type in tints. Such was used here to set large page numbers in the background behind the text.

Using Two Colors

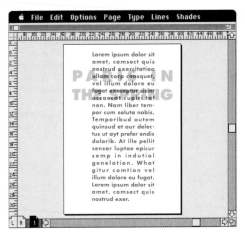

Using certain color combinations will allow both colors to be visible and legible at the same time. By choosing two colors carefully and instructing your printer to overprint inks, a third color can be obtained.

The color system developed by printers uses the three subtractive primaries of cyan (near blue), magenta (near red) and yellow, as well as the standard black. Most page-makeup software has these facilities, and if you have a color monitor, these can be displayed on screen. Of course you can choose to use any color or combination of colors, as long as you can provide the printer with separated artwork (ie, artwork for each color that will print) and with a color swatch (sample) of each of the colors required.

Color is an important tool in the language of graphics, but it is still a relatively expensive option, because each color that you specify in your artwork has to be printed separately.

The cheapest way to use color is to print a normal black and white design onto colored paper. This need not be merely decorative, it can have a practical function, because it allows the designer to color code the different sections of a publication.

Black and white page spreads can be enhanced enormously by the addition of an extra color, but care should be taken when specifying lightly toned colors (like yellow and pastel tints) especially for small point sizes of text. Legibility depends on the contrast between the colors of paper and ink, and the more you deviate from the highest contrast of black and white, the less legible the text will become.

CHECK**LIST**

- Use an overlay for the second color artwork.

- Attach a swatch of the color you require, or specify a Pantone color number.

- Make sure the overlay and flat artwork have corresponding registration marks.

- Colors can be printed solid or in halftone tints.

- Don't use very lightly toned colors for small point sizes of type.

- Remember that you can't print light colors over darker ones.

- Aim for tonal contrast between your two colors.

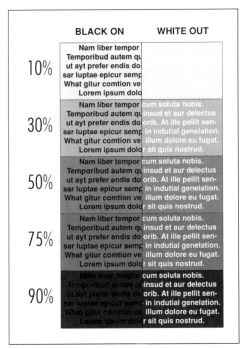

Judging tints takes a great deal of experience. Laser-printers tend to image tints darker due to dot spread. The linotronic image of the same element will tend to lighten the image due to its high definition of dot, but this can be affected by the resolution of screen used. When the printer shoots a bromide tint, the grayness of the tint can vary either way according to his camera settings. Finally, offset-litho printing should lighten the tint if the machine is inked correctly. However, over-inking (to get good blacks) will darken a tint.

Color can be an effective way to highlight a few words within a passage. But use it carefully. It will stand out more than italicizing text and it will interrupt the reader's flow.

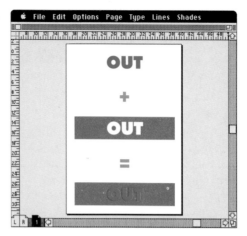

This is very simple separated artwork. Since the text could not overprint on a block of solid color it has been "knocked out" of the block. Current DTP packages will handle this type of separation.

Although green is a secondary (ie, derived) color, it has the appearance of being a new color, much more than orange or purple, the other two derived colors.

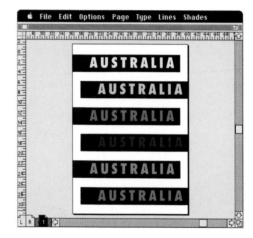

Colors have tonal values equivalent to the amount of light or dark within them. In order for the type to be legible there must be suffcient tonal contrast between the background and the type.

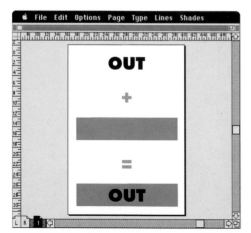

When overprinting black or any darker tone on top of a lighter color, there is usually no need to reverse out the text from its background.

Even two colors can be used in a creative way to capture the purpose of a layout. Using a second color as a tint behind text is a useful way to enliven a copy-heavy page, where there is no room to dedicate an area to graphics.

Using Full Color

B y overprinting the three primaries, which are cyan, magenta and yellow, a wide range of secondary and tertiary colors can be produced, and when these are in turn overprinted with the fourth color, black, to enrich the tonal contrast, full-color (also called four-color) printing results. Four-color process printing is used for the artwork that includes color illustrations or photographs. Color artwork has to be photographed or scanned to produce four-color separated printing plates, one for each of the printed colors. During this process the image is screened and converted into halftone dots, which have to be differently oriented on each plate to derive maximum benefit from overprinting, and to avoid undesirable moiré, or dot, patterns.

Full- or four-color printing adds enormous impact to published material, but it can be badly used and overused. If you are going to order expensive color printing, then it is extremely important to make sure that your design really optimizes the use of color.

Color can be more effective if it is used sparingly and with discretion. Take the example of a travel brochure. These booklets are often packed with full-color photographs – so packed that in fact the eye is saturated with color, reducing the impact of any individual image. Compare this with an exhibition catalogue of paintings that features color images each on a separate page, with wide margins to isolate the image in a restful white space.

Don't feel limited to black and white for text. Experiment with legible process tints which can be output as separations from high-resolution imagesetters.

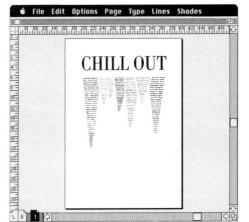

Cool colors have been used to enhance the effect of icicles in this layout.

Warm colors are those that tend towards red and yellow.

Color can be used like a graphic to break up columns of text, and make starting and ending points visible.

Color on a DTP system allows you to be much more creative with illustration. Here a graphic is laid in a tint to alleviate the grayness of a page of type. This effect can also be used on photographs, printing at less than full strength of image.

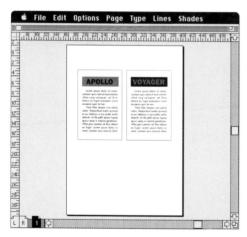

Strong red colors appear to advance or come closer, while blue and cold colors tend to recede.

When using type over a colored background, you should decide whether to use black-on type, or white-out for maximum legibility.

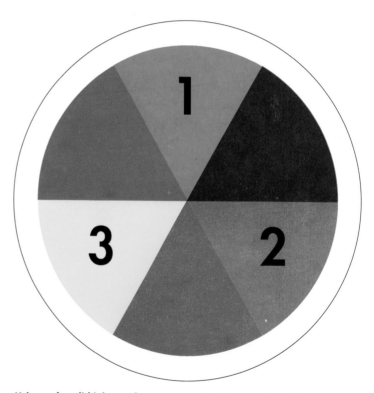

Using only solid inks, and no percentage tints, a good variety of different colors can be achieved. The three process colors, cyan (1), magenta (2) and yellow (3), are usually printed along with black in most full-color printing. From these colors you can achieve virtually any other. Colors on your computer screen are created from red, green and blue light sources and this difference will cause problems when trying to model colors for later separated output.

Tabulation

Tabulation is the presentation of information (words and figures) in the form of tables or lists – like menus and price lists. When preparing tabulation the designer is acting very specifically as an information processor. He or she must make sometimes complex data under-standable and readable when it is present-ed on the page.

The designer is guided by two fac-tors: first, by how the data can be grouped into different classifications and thus rep-resented by different typographic treat-ment; and secondly, how this information can be laid out on the page. Menus for example are generally presented as two tabular columns – a list of the menu items on the left and a list of related prices on the right. It is the designer's job to make these two lists relate to each other so that the customer has no problem in finding the price for any of the choices available. Traditional layouts for different types of lists should be carefully considered; they have survived because they are very effi-cient!

Two tabulated columns can be made to relate in a variety of ways: by close spacing and layout, by using leaders (rows of dots or symbols linking both columns horizontally), by complementary ranging of type (setting the two columns back to back by ranging them left and right), or by using rules and boxes to separate the list-ed items.

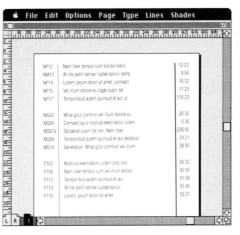

When you are setting tables of text one of the most important things is to make columns easily distinguishable from each other. In this example intercolumn rules were used.

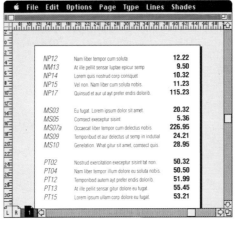

In this example, columns were set in different typestyles. Some programs will let you vertically select a row and apply a format to it. Otherwise you have to skip through, applying styles line by line.

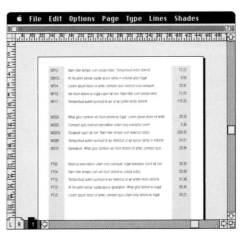

Another technique for distinguishing columns is the use of a secondary color, either as a tint over-lay or the color of text itself. This is a favorite technique for annual reports.

◆ CHECK**LIST**

- Separate the copy into logical categories.

- Decide how many columns you will need.

- Check the longest entry for each column to ascertain the column width.

- Make sure that related items in separate tabulated columns can be easily understood by the reader.

- Use leaders to connect related items from one col-umn to another.

- Use different typefaces or variants to separate differ-ent categories of informa-tion.

- Use complementary type ranging to relate columns of information.

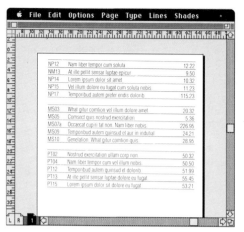

As well as vertical columns, the reader must easily be able to follow horizontal rows. In this instance horizontal rules have been used to lead the eye. Spreadsheet programs can be useful for typesetting tables like this that can then be captured as graphics and placed in a page makeup program.

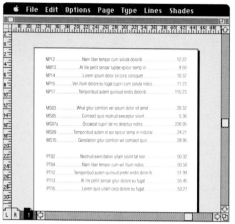

This traditional format of ranged-left text, followed by center tab, followed by a ranged-right tab allows the maximum evenness of space between items but looks slightly ragged down the central column.

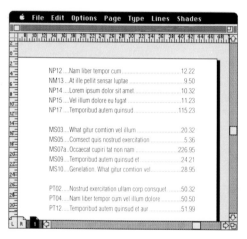

Tab leader dots are devices that lead the eye across rows of text where the gaps may be unequal, or perhaps a little too long to follow easily. An alternative is to underscore your text or add horizontal rules.

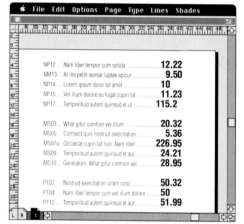

Decimal tabs are useful if you are setting price lists or invoices where you need the decimal points to line up. To add to this you should use a monospaced font so the columns of type will also line up.

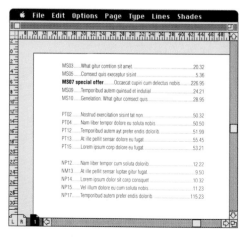

When using tabs, don't let your layout be ruined by one abnormally long entry. Simply space it manually, using periods if you are employing tab leader dots.

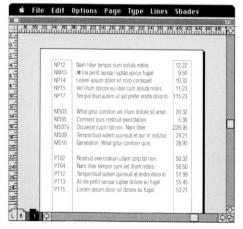

When using multiple-column layouts, you may find it more useful to set the individual columns in separate boxes within your DTP program. This allows you more control over the items within each column, rather than the items line by line as most programs interpret text.

Choosing the Right Image

Flat colour

Woodcut

Typeset text is a linear medium, revealing its content over a period of time, as it is read. In contrast, images are iconic – instantly appraised by the viewer. The power of images – as a means of instantly communicating ideas that in text would be laborious – can be exploited only if we understand when, how and where they are best used.

The illustration of an idea can take a wide variety of forms – from a thumbnail sketch or sketchmap, to a technical illustration, oil painting or photograph – and it is important to consider the medium and style of the image (is it a style that is relevant to the text? – will this medium reproduce well on my DTP system?), as well as its content.

When you have a shortlist of ideas, you have to decide whether you can produce a suitable illustration yourself, or if you should commission an artist, or specify an image to a picture researcher, or whether you should use a "ready-made" (non-copyright) image. Collections of "clip art" can be useful.

Painting software for micro-computers has already reached a quality and resolution that a few years ago was impossible to produce with mainframes, and both bit-mapped and object-oriented packages have originated styles of their own, as well as being able to replicate most traditional media.

Crayon

Watercolour

Airbrush

Computer

The style of an illustration is a product of the image content and of the technique used to produce it. Choosing the right style depends on your assessment of the context of the illustration – the author's message embodied in the text, and the type of audience/readership the message is aimed at. There are no hard rules here – sometimes the style of illustration can reinforce the message, sometimes it can counterpoint it. Flat color gives an effect like an animated cartoon image – very hard edge, young and modern. Woodcuts are traditional, folksy, primitive and bold. Crayons are soft and feminine. Watercolors are more delicate and subtle. Airbrush gives a very masculine, technical, hard edge image, while computer paint programs produce a very rich textural image, in many respects like that of a woven fabric or tapestry.

Different illustration styles can work well with certain styles of type. Here the semi-bold sans serif has been chosen to visually match the dominant black outlines of the flat color image.

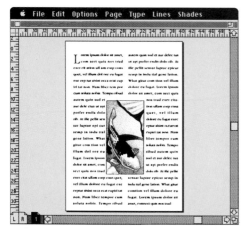

The stipple technique is capable of very fine, almost photographic effects, and demands a suitably fine typographic treatment, and works well with this classical serif face. The text has been well linespaced leaded to further enhance the tonal balance between image and text.

The much bolder style and black lines of the woodcut demands plenty of white space as a balance. The text typeface has a good black letter effect, set justified to form a matching rectangle, while tighter leading and the bold drop cap give the text an appropriate darker tone.

When you commission illustrations, you must specify not only the general content and the technique you require, but also the finished dimensions and orientation (whether it's landscape or portrait). Then the illustrator can decide whether to make the illustration "same size" (s/s) or larger than required ("twice up" or "half up"), so that when it's reduced (photographically as a PMT bromide, or by scanning), a finely detailed image is produced. You shouldn't use commissioned illustrations larger than the original artwork size because, as you can see here, the enlarged drawing can be coarsely defined, and the intended range of tonality is lost.

Positioning Images/1

This final stage involves the scaling, cropping, framing and positioning of the image on the page. Care should be taken in choosing an appropriate scale for the illustration. Some subtlety is possible here – for instance, the scale of the image content (whether it's a landscape or the close-up of an eye, for example) may be purposely reversed (a large image of the eye, a miniature of the landscape) so that some drama occurs when they are displayed on the same page or spread. Cropping, in conjunction with copy and paste functions, can also be very useful, allowing the sequential enlargements of relevant detail, or the staccato repetition of detail, or the repetition of an illustration, to link text through a number of pages.

The layout of images on a page depends as much on the content of the pictures as on their shape and tone. In the first section of the book we saw how simple blocks of text can affect the page layout through their tonal value, and the same is true of image blocks. Illustrations and photographs can be delicate or heavy, according to their overall qualities of dark and light tones. With images, though, the content of the picture can take on an importance overriding tonal considerations. For example, a photograph of the profile of a man walking can be positioned so that he appears to be walking on to the page, across the page, or off the edge of the page. Each one of these alternatives should be considered in relation to the text content, as well as the overall layout.

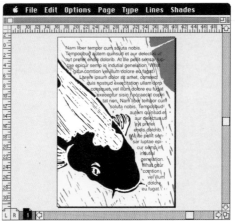

The very defined edge of this image made it a natural choice for a runaround. First an outline of the image had to be put on to the computer, which in this case was done by scanning. However the final image was dropped in by the printer.

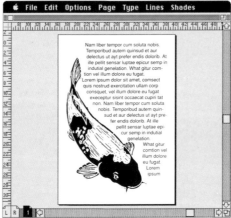

Here the type was run around the important part of the image but the rest of the image was not cropped.

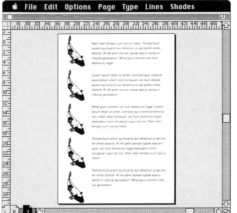

This effect of simply duplicating the image is a way to make the best of very low-quality material. It adds a modern feel to the layout, like a video clip.

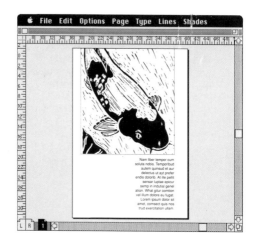

The content of your image may give you ideas about position and cropping. Here the fish has been bled off the top of the page as if it were swimming downwards. The reader's eye is thus led into the type.

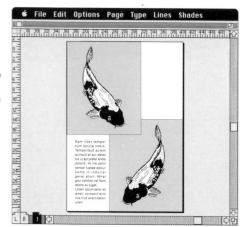

To aid this composition, the image was flipped over, which is something you can get away with on images that contain no text.

A modern design technique is to reduce images to almost postage stamp size. This can have a very pleasing aesthetic effect, especially when plenty of space is then left on the page. But it can be frustrating for the viewer who wants to see detail.

This "wall of video" layout is offset by simple centered text.

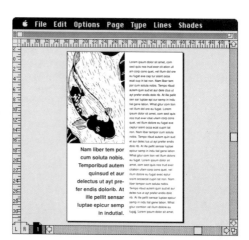

Bleeding the fish in from a corner of the page works well with the composition of the image and leads comfortably into the opening paragraph of text.

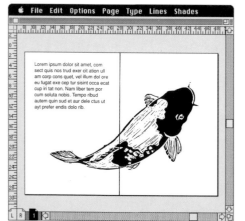

A double-page bleed like this is the most dramatic use of images. When reversing text out be careful it doesn't cross over an area of white in the picture and become illegible.

Positioning Images/2

 CHECK**LIST**

As we have mentioned, image layout is an editorial as well as an aesthetic concern, and this is especially true for journalistic layouts such as newsletters and newspapers, where image and text combine to tell a story. For example, with portrait photographs or illustrations make sure that the image is positioned so that the subject appears to be looking into the centre of interest of the spread or towards the accompanying text or title, not arbitrarily looking away off the edge of the page.

There is an increasingly wide range of image manipulation features available with DTP systems, and these can be used to enliven spreads even where there is only minimal image copy available. Images can be repeated, each repeat successively zooming in on the main detail of the image. Images can be inverted to a negative, flipped to give a mirror image, copied and cropped to focus attention on a detail. They can also be copied and progressively distorted to give an expressive effect; autotraced to reduce a bitmapped image to an outline drawing and so on. One of the most exciting aspects of working in this new medium is experimenting with these possibilities, combining a variety of different effects to see what happens. But however much you experiment, remember that the ultimate effect must be to elucidate the content of the copy and/or to decorate it in a relevant style.

- Let the content help you decide the most effective position for the image.

- Remember that in DTP bleed is effective from the edge of the non-printing margin, not from the edge of the paper.

- Use a typeface relevant to functions to produce repeats.

- Progressive distortions of the same image can produce dynamic effects.

- Try reversing text out of suitably dark toned images.

- Use the content of the image to direct the reader's eye to the main text or title.

- Vignetting an image can be done in a paint program.

- Make sure you leave an even margin of white space when text is wrapping an image.

- Autotrace drawings can be very effective alongside bitmapped images.

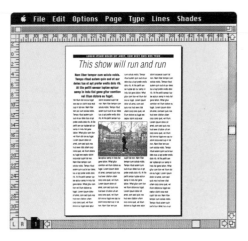

In this layout the photograph breaks up the body text but seems isolated in the middle of the page, like a pull quote.

This more natural layout allows the photo to bleed off the side of the page. However now the bottom half of the page looks pretty dull.

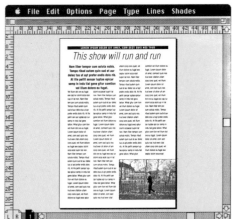

This layout allows the photo to bleed off the lower edge. Now the page has a more even distribution of elements on it with the bold paragraph at the top matching the photo at the bottom.

Bleeding a photograph across a central gutter is generally not a good idea. This layout also breaks the text flow in the middle of the page, and the reader's eye becomes confused as to where to continue.

Positioning these two photographs at diagonally opposite corners of the spread allows as much space as possible between them and leaves a clear path for the text to be easily followed through without the reader's eye having to avoid obstacles.

The photographs are placed on the right-hand side of this spread in an attempt to balance the heading. However their different shapes make the layout seem miscalculated.

Tilting photos is a complicated process with current DTP packages, requiring the keyline box for the design to be drawn in a separate package and imported. This is one reason why it's better to design with pen and paper; you don't have to compromise what you want by what you can easily do.

Moving the heading allows the pictures to be laid out more logically. Both start at the same point down from the top of the page, so some kind of uniformity is imposed on the layout.

If you are scanning photographs and producing finished artwork direct from your DTP system, you have much more control over the image and can use effects that are impossible conventionally, such as this stretched-out eye.

SECTION TWO
DTP in Action

In the introductory section we described the design process that most designers will use to tackle a graphics problem, and in the following examples you will see how the designer actually formulates ideas, tests them in different versions and develops them to finished "soft" artwork.

DESIGNER AS IMAGE MAKER

What we can't easily illustrate in this book is the "invisible" process of design – how you define a particular graphics problem and originate preliminary ideas before you start roughing them out in visual form. This process happens when a designer's knowledge, experience and intuition interact together to produce a series of mental images of design possibilities. When these are visually tested as thumbnails and working roughs, this invisible process continues, with the designer applying his common sense, his experience of layout and typefaces and his knowledge of graphics processes in order to direct his skills as an image maker.

Everyone has the natural abilities required to become a designer, but becoming a good graphic designer requires that you make a study of those elements that will enable you to perform this invisible process well. You have begun this process by exploring DTP and by reading this book. Apart from DTP technique, the next essential prerequisite is some knowledge of graphic design history, which for this purpose can be viewed as a catalogue of how other designers have tackled graphic design problems within the prevailing technical, social and cultural conditions of their time. Some study of the history of graphics, including contemporary work, will also help you realize that designers do not operate in a vacuum, that they are part of an ongoing process, intricately bound up with society and its cultural life.

The ability to think visually depends upon having some means of rapidly illustrating your ideas, and you should make every attempt to develop your drawing skills, practicing first of all by sketching different letter forms and typefaces. You don't need to be a brilliant draftsman or illustrator, in fact many graphic designers can't draw in the academic sense. But you will need to develop a shorthand method of sketching layouts and typefaces in rough so that exploratory design alternatives can be quickly assessed before you start on your DTP system.

A KNOWLEDGE OF TYPEFACES

Another essential asset is a knowledge of typefaces – how they are used and what effect they have as devices for the communication of ideas. This is another good reason for studying graphic design history, as many of the faces we use today, ones such as Times, Helvetica, Baskerville and Bodoni, are themselves important historical landmarks (these four faces span the last three centuries). You should also develop your awareness of how letter forms and typefaces are used by professional designers in everyday items, such as advertisements, magazines, packaging and newspapers. Build up a scrapbook of examples of lettering and typography that you admire and examine these carefully by identifying the typefaces, drawing them and by attempting to reproduce similar effects in your own system. A scrapbook will become an invaluable reference resource, and can also be used as an ideas generating tool. As you get to know typefaces you will find that each design has an individual personality that is suggested by its shape, the way it works as a block of text, and its general style, and this knowledge will help you select exactly the right face for each job.

PHOTOGRAPHS AND ILLUSTRATIONS

In your study of graphic design, you will also need to build up a knowledge of images and the techniques that are used to produce and reproduce them. Illustration and photography are an integral part of graphic design, and when combined with typography provide the three main communication tools available to the designer. Images can communicate com-plex information very quickly and effectively, and the choice of the style of image (whether it's a photo, oil painting, potato cut, etc) can either reinforce or detract from this communication process. Often photographic images will contain all sorts of information that is not relevant to the central point that you are trying to make, and if you are not careful this incidental information can carry contradictory or confusing messages for the reader. Just as you are collecting samples of letter forms and typefaces, start collecting examples of various photographs and illustrations that you think are good examples of images used to communicate ideas and add these to your graphics scrapbook.

Finally you will need to know more about the reproduction techniques used in printing and how these can be utilized effectively in the design process. You will already know something about what laserprinters can do, and often this is sufficient, but if you are planning long runs or require color printing, then you will have to know more about artwork production for the offset litho print process. This aspect is covered briefly in the final section, "Beyond the Screen".

Creating Logos

SIMON ✚ SIMON

Above. Simon & Simon are book publishers. They require a logo that has a classic look, but with an added hint of modernity. The ampersand (itself a ligature or logotype meaning "and") suggested a suitable starting point from which to explore a range of designs. The repeated family name will also be a major feature in the design. Replacing the ampersand with a modern plus sign and making this into a symbol by reversing it out of a black circle offsets the classical roman typeface.

✦ CHECK**LIST**

- Logos can be made up of letters, shapes and images.

- Keep images simple to insure that they are legible over a wide range of reproduction sizes.

- Use standard and etymological dictionaries, encyclopedias and the thesaurus to research the company name and help you generate ideas.

- Create a file of typeface examples that seem to be relevant to the name and style of the company.

- Look for metaphors and analogies suggested by the company name and mode of business.

- Maintain a collection of symbols, special type devices and pictograms.

Logos can be made up of letters, words, or images (or all three), and are used as a graphic device to symbolize a company or institution. Just as a national flag symbolizes a country, the logo should represent a company and graphically express its character and style. The idea for the logo can be derived in a variety of ways: from a typographic treatment of the company's name (as in the case of Simon and Simon), or of its initials; from a typographic treatment of the meaning or implied meaning of the company's name (as in Pento); or from a pictorial treatment of the latter.

Symbols condense or compress meaning and represent that meaning in a simple graphic image. The history of visual communications is replete with symbols. They are a useful visual shorthand and can be integrated within a logo to imply a much larger message or connote a particular style or association (as in TransAtlantic).

Letterforms are symbols, too, of course and here the application of a suitable typeface is of the utmost importance. The type chosen for a logo will provide the viewer with a subtle identifier, a subliminal message, that can express authority, modernity, speed, or in the case of the famous IBM logo (designed by Paul Rand in the 50s) the whole area of computation.

Below. With DTP you can create your own versions of ampersands. Here we've used Futura Book. Thin rules tie in the enlarged ampersand.

SIMON **&** SIMON

Right. The same typeface used with an exotic ampersand – the calligraphic flourishes contrast well with the modern classic face.

SIMON *&* SIMON

SIMON *&* SIMON

Above. The exotic set against the roman typeface – perhaps this is too traditionally classical?

SIMON & SIMON

Left. By reversing the scale of typeface to ampersand and stressing the repeated names by vertically stacking them one over the other, a more integrated logo emerges.

Right. Double box rules enhance the white space that encloses the type and give the impression of a book plate or spine label, though there is some ambiguity in this idea – it could be a perfume label.

SIMON & SIMON

Right. A horizontal rule reinforces the two separate names and emphasizes the central ampersand.

SIMON & SIMON PARIS

Left. The ligature "section" or double "S" serves three functions. It is a device traditionally associated with books (as a reference mark); it relates visually to the ampersand, and it echoes the double "S" initials of the company name.

Left. A small image is used to accentuate the nature of the business and is a reminder of the distinguishing trademarks or colophons that are traditionally used by publishers. OK, maybe this is obvious, but logos should communicate simply.

PENTO
PRODUCTIONS

Left. There are some more basic ways of combining the two words of the company name. Pento is the most important element, and because it's a shorter word it can easily be increased in size. It's difficult to get a hard, vertical lefthand edge when the first word ends in an "O" – a rectangular box solves this problem, but there's no hint of a film business.

PENTO PRODUCTIONS

Left. This film and video company quite definitely didn't want any hint of a filmstrip in their logo! So we've taken the dictionary definition of the root word (from the Greek penta = five) as a starting point. This gives us plenty of opportunity for a rich variety of graphic treatments. Handled like this, the broken pentagon suggests expansion or radiation. The extra bold typeface works well with the heavy chevrons.

Below. We've also got two "P"s to play with in the company title. Repetition of a graphic symbol or character often works, but this looks very cramped and the white spaces are ugly. The circular frame explores other ways of suggesting "5" – but beware of unintended associations; this could look like a life belt!

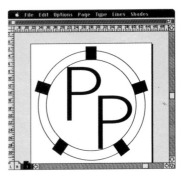

Left. Several paint programs allow the possibility of setting type to a curvilinear baseline. This has a very light-hearted effect here and is balanced by the modern feel of the well letterspaced "Productions." The fine horizontal rules add the necessary structure, allowing the logo to be positioned in such a way that it relates to the page edges.

★ PENTO PRODUCTIONS

Left. The five-pointed star also carries strong American or show-biz connotations. By using the same typeface in two different sizes and ranging the two lines to the same measure, the logo is given an integrated feel – but there's an unhappy white space around the star.

Background. This treatment works well as a stand-alone symbol – the circular frame echoes the shape of a film projection reel. Prepare several suitable components for the logo first, then use the computer to try various typefaces and styles, juxtaposing all these elements to see what works best.

Below. Well, you've got to start somewhere! The most obvious ideas can sometimes work (TransAtlantic is a shipping firm). It's a good idea to sketch them out, because even if they are clichéd and clumsy they may spark another idea. At this stage in the design process all ideas-generating techniques are useful.

Left. Another obvious idea – maps are intrinsically interesting and amenable to all sorts of graphic treatments, but this makes the long company name even bulkier. How would it reproduce in miniature? Note the movement implied in the slanted italics. You can see the designer trying to solve this graphic problem – starting with the most obvious pictorial associations and working up a more subtle treatment as we progress through this series of logo designs.

TRANSATLANTIC

Left. Here we've tried to cope with the long name by using a very condensed face – the vertical, exaggerated serifs help counterpoint the horizontal span of the word. The stylized globe is very recognizable, and symbolizes (rather than illustrating) the meaning inherent in the company name.

Right. This is beginning to work. The more realistic globe image is now integrated with the type. Splitting the word into two parts and two styles serves to visually compress it, while at the same time the idea of movement is expressed in the italic component.

Trans Atlantic

*Trans*Atlantic

Above. Another visual symbol strongly associated with shipping – the International Code of Signals flags. We try two against the globe to see how they might work. The "Tr" and "sA" in the typesetting have been kerned to give a better fit.

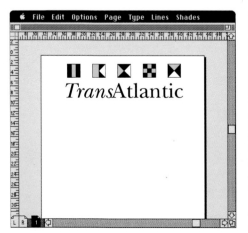

Left. Adding the flags for "T" and "A" and spacing them to fill the text measure give a much more unified design, with type and images firmly linked together. Word spacing has been removed and kerning altered on the "Tr". We have the implied movement, the company name is now a unity, images are decorative and relevant – an elegant solution.

Designing Letterheads

Below. This very cool treatment combines logo and type components well – the shape of the card is emphasized by the way type is ranged-right and by the upper and left edges of the logo rectangle. Lavish use of white space gives a very elegant and sophisticated appearance.

Letterheads and business cards are on the one hand functional tools for identifying the facts of name, address, phone number, etc, and as a vehicle for correspondence. On the other hand they are the primary method of graphically establishing the company's style and purpose.

The designer must consider the function of letterheads first – they have to include sufficient empty space for written, typed or printed-out letters. There are functional and perhaps legal requirements for what must appear on the letterhead. These will certainly include name, address and phone number, but may also include Telex and Fax number, list of company officers, etc. The letterhead is most likely going to be printed as hard copy, but would a soft letterhead – a template held on hard disk – also be useful?

Other considerations of functionality include: use of a standard paper size (or not, if there's a good design argument for not doing so); designing for standard envelope sizes; possible use of window envelopes, address labels, continuous stationery (for printouts); how well the design photocopies; how the color of paper used responds to typists' corrections, how it prints in a laserprinter.

For a range of stationery you will need to develop a basic grid layout so that all the various components of the range all graphically relate to, and reinforce, each other.

Right. Extra leading extends the address to occupy a rectangle, balancing the logo. Note the use of a superscript character in the abbreviation of "street." There's a good structuring of information (logo, address, director's name) in this layout.

Left. This example of the card design incorporates two new ideas – using an unusual vertical format facilitates centering of the design, which, in conjunction with rules surrounding the address, gives the card a more modern feel, while maintaining its classical layout.

Below. This layout for the letterhead allows plenty of room for addressee and date information at top left, and for the bulk of the letter text at center left. The logo, address and list of directors occupies an elegantly long and narrow column – look at how the fine horizontal interline rules provide a visual connection with the logo and the paper edges.

SIMON
&
SIMON

• 17 STANDFORD ST • LONDON W4 1SF • TEL (01) 995 6874 • TELEX 997123 TELEX D •

SIMON
&
SIMON

17 STANDFORD ST
LONDON W4 1SF
TEL (01) 995 6874
TELEX 997123 TELEX D

ATRICK SIMON • RONALD SIMON • EMMA PRITCHARD • RICHARD JEFFRIES •

Directors:
PATRICK SIMON
RONALD SIMON
EMMA PRITCHARD
RICHARD JEFFRIES

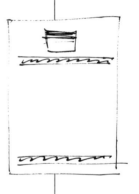

Above. Instead of implying the space for letter writing, this layout encloses the space in long horizontal rules. Centering the type and logo makes for a much more traditional, more authoritative design that is very elegant.

Below. There are certain basic functions that the business card must perform, including communicating the company name, address and phone number, and the name of the officer or employee carrying the card. The card can also say something about the company's style. Here we've used a repetition of the logo with the solid and tinted versions to add a 3-dimensional quality to the design.

Harold W. Stafford
President

Pento Productions
112 Monson Avenue

Marietta

GA 30062

610-777-2121

Above. These are simply the most important elements placed in the computer program to allow you to judge how much copy and space you have to juggle with.

Right. In this version the two text components: the president's name and title, and the company name and address are separated, allowing the bottom line of ranged-left text to firmly anchor the design to the card edges.

Harold W. Stafford

President

Pento Productions

112 Monson Avenue, Marietta, GA 30062, 610-777-2121

Left. The text has been bound to a wavy line (called a "spline") to try to give the appearance of film running off the reel. Space has been added between all characters to cover up kerning inconsistencies.

Pento Productions: 112 Monson Avenue, Marietta, GA 30062, 610-777-2121
Partners: Harold W. Stafford, Patricia Cannon, Maxfield Marshall, Ursula Green, David Jeffrey Mann

Above. The large offset and tinted logo provides a unifying structure for the letterhead, with a reworked version of the logo top center, its shape pointing down to the address and list of executives at the foot of the page. The tinted background is OK for computer printouts of letters, but hard for a secretary to correct errors from a typewriter.

Above. Much more aggressively dynamic! The final choice of the sort of stylistic message the letterhead projects is of course up to the client. It's the designer's job to guide the client in making that choice, by pointing out the pros and cons of alternative treatments.

Right. By skewing all the elements like this, a very state-of-the-art effect is achieved. This is legible, and perfect for a client company involved in the youth orientated pop video market, but perhaps unsuitable (too excessive) for an established, multi-faceted production company. Paint and font manipulation programs provide the DTP designer with the sort of tools previously only available (at enormous expense!) at specialist photo typesetting companies.

Designing Invoices

These items should be seen as part of a range of stationery designs and so share the overall styling of the main letterhead and business card, but they also have special functional considerations in that they serve a vital role in the successful management of the company's finances. Invoices and price lists may have to be made out by various people within the company, and great efforts should be made to determine what is useful to them. If there is an existing range of stationery, what do the users feel about that? The visual aspect of the design must grow out of the paper's function and it should make the invoice easier to use or the price list easier to update, as well as graphically fitting into the wider stationery style.

The style of stationery should likewise grow out of what the company does – or would like to do. This requires some degree of subtlety from the designer, as in many cases the most obvious solution can be too obvious (a cliché). Clichés can be a very valuable shorthand, but non-obvious solutions should be explored as well. Good stationery will express typographically both the nature of the business the company engages in and the way in which that business is transacted.

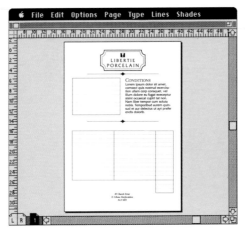

Left. The client required an elegant, late nineteenth century feel for its invoices. The first step was to develop the logo, and Victorian decorative box rules were used to frame the company name. But this initial layout is unclear. What goes in which box? How do you know it's an invoice?

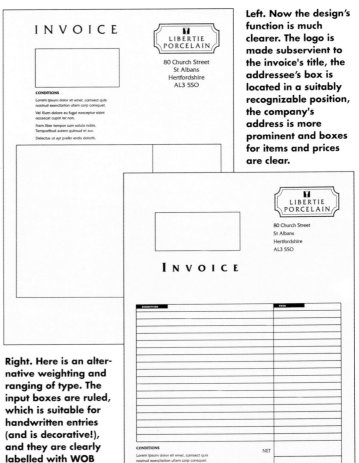

Left. Now the design's function is much clearer. The logo is made subservient to the invoice's title, the addressee's box is located in a suitably recognizable position, the company's address is more prominent and boxes for items and prices are clear.

Right. Here is an alternative weighting and ranging of type. The input boxes are ruled, which is suitable for handwritten entries (and is decorative!), and they are clearly labelled with WOB panels. But the conditions text is still not properly integrated.

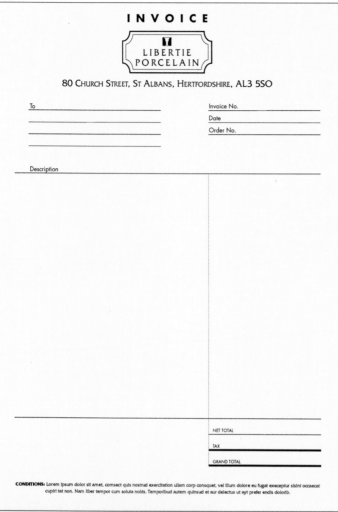

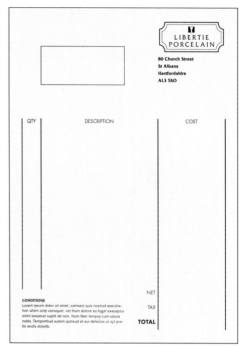

Right. This nearly works, and demonstrates how minimal the use of boxes and rules can be. But the box for the client's address floats a little unhappily. Again the conditions text fills the unused space well. There is again no invoice title!

Left. A centered layout gives a more accurate period feel. All the input panels are labeled, using a small point size sans serif. The fact that there are no guide rules for input of items and prices leaves clean white spaces in the design. Note the clear hierarchy of information.

Left. Here is the ultimate in stylish minimalism – OK if you don't write invoices very often! There is no identifying title, no guide rules to position the input of the supplier's address, items and prices, and the conditions text is too prominent. It's very smart in a 1930s sense but not functional enough.

Left. This invoice has an aggressively modern styling with a strong asymmetrical hanging box, positioned with heavy horizontal rules. But there are too many input boxes competing with the logo and no mention of an invoice title. Note how the conditions text fills an otherwise unused part of the layout.

Order Forms and Price Lists

As with other items in the stationery range that exist as vehicles for people to add things to, the order form should be designed expressly with the user in mind. This entails researching the way in which the order form will be used and designing a graphic structure that will cater to every probable contingency and variety of input. Make a list of the items to appear on the order form. These will include, as basics, the name, address, and telephone number of the sender; space for similar data about the receiver; columns for the quantity, catalogue identification, type, price and sales tax of goods ordered; and some ruled lines to separate this information, with spaces indicated for total costs, etc. Be sure that you know how the forms will be filled in by the user, as the layout must allow suitable space for keyboard or handwritten entries.

Price lists have to be considered on two levels: First, there must be a logical and coherent layout so that the recipient can easily relate items, parts numbers and prices (including tax where necessary). Secondly, the design must be relevant and suitable to the client's business and to the intended customer. Tabulated columns of items and prices must be arranged coherently, by means of typographical treatment (easily related styles of type), by layout or by means of leaders. (Leaders are lines of dots or other graphic symbols that fill in the space between the item and price, visually leading the eye from one to the other.)

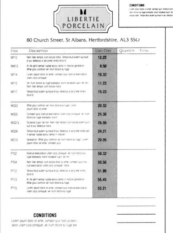

Right. Extend the logo with horizontal rules and you lead the eye to the form's title. The items are clearly described and priced but what are the three columns of boxes for? Remember that an order form is filled in by the customer so input positions must be clearly labelled. The conditions text floats like an afterthought.

Left. Now we have clear, descriptive labels for each column, and the unit costs are highlighted in a tinted panel. The centered logo and address conform to the required period feel, but there's no mention that this is an order form, and the conditions text needs to be repositioned to conform to the layout grid.

Right. This asymmetrical version has a clear title in well letterspaced italic serif. The very functional layout has the items classified under general headings. Horizontal guidelines do help where there's a detailed tabulated list to cross relate. Now the conditions text is integrated with the layout.

ORDER FORM

LIBERTIE PORCELAIN

DESC		RRP	NABUS EST	FOGOR EST	TOTAL
Nam liber tempor cum soluta nobis. Temporibud autem quinsud et aur delectus ut ayt prefer endis dolorib. At ille pellit sensar luptae epicur semp in indutial genelation. What gitur comtion vel illum dolore eu fugat.		12.22			
Nam liber tempor cum soluta nobis. Temporibud autem quinsud et aur delectus ut ayt prefer endis dolorib. At ille pellit sensar luptae epicur semp in indutial genelation. What gitur comtion vel illum dolore eu fugat.		9.50			
Nam liber tempor cum soluta nobis. Temporibud autem quinsud et aur delectus ut ayt prefer endis dolorib. At ille pellit sensar luptae epicur semp in indutial genelation. What gitur comtion vel illum dolore eu fugat.		10.32			
Nam liber tempor cum soluta nobis. Temporibud autem quinsud et aur delectus ut ayt prefer endis dolorib. At ille pellit sensar luptae epicur semp in indutial genelation. What gitur comtion vel illum dolore eu fugat.		11.23			
Nam liber tempor cum soluta nobis. Temporibud autem quinsud et aur delectus ut ayt prefer endis dolorib. At ille pellit sensar luptae epicur semp in indutial genelation. What gitur comtion vel illum dolore eu fugat.		15.23			

INSTRUCTIONS

Nam liber tempor cum soluta nobis. Temporibud autem quinsud et aur delectus ut ayt prefer endis dolorib.

At ille pellit sensar luptae epicur semp in indutial genelation. What gitur comtion vel illum dolore eu fugat.

Lorem ipsum dolor sit amet, comsect quis nostrud exercitation ullam corp consquet, vel illum dolore.

Eu fugat execeptur sisint occaecat cupiri tat non. Nam liber tempor cum soluta nobis.

Temporibud autem quinsud et aur delectus ut ayt prefer endis dolorib. At ille pellit sensar luptae epicur semp in indutial genelation.

GRAND TOTAL

SEND TO
80 CHURCH ST,
ST ALBANS,
HERTFORDSHIRE,
AL3 5SO

LIBERTIE PORCELAIN *Order Form*
80 Church Street, St Albans, Hertfordshire, AL3 5SO

VESSELS

Nam liber tempor cum soluta nobis. Temporibud autem quinsud et aur delectus ut ayt prefer endis dolorib. At ille pellit sensar luptae epicur semp in indutial genelation. What gitur comtion vel illum dolore eu fugat. **Unit RRP 12.22**		
Lorem ipsum dolor sit amet, comsect quis nostrud exercitation ullam corp consquet. Vel illum dolore eu fugat execeptur sisint occaecat cupiri tat non. Nam liber tempor cum soluta nobis. **Unit RRP 9.50**		
Temporibud autem quinsud et aur delectus ut ayt prefer endis dolorib. What gitur comtion vel illum dolore eu fugat. Lorem ipsum dolor sit amet. **Unit RRP 10.32**		
Comsect quis nostrud exercitation ullam corp consquet, vel illum dolore eu fugat execeptur sisint. Occaecat cupiri tat non. Nam liber tempor cum soluta nobis autem quinsud et aur delectus nobis **Unit RRP 11.23**		
Temporibud autem quinsud et aur delectus ut ayt prefer endis pellit sensar luptae epicur semp in indutial Genelation. What gitur comtion vel illum dolore eu fugat. Lorem ipsum dolor sit amet, comsect quis **Unit RRP 15.23**		

CONDITIONS
Lorem ipsum dolor sit amet, comsect quis nostrud exerc sisint occaecat cupiri tat non. At ille pellit sensar luptae epicur semp in indutial. Temporibud autem quinsud et aur delectus ut ayt prefer endis dolorib

Above. Perhaps this comes closer than the other approaches to combining the period style of the logo and order form title with the modern functionality of illustration, product description and price list. This layout works for a limited number of product types but is too unwieldy for long listings.

Above. Here is a more obviously commercial approach – but is it the style right for Libertie? Functionally this works well, with simple pictograms to illustrate the basic styles of ceramic product. The "Morse code" vertical rule adds a sense of urgency, leading the eye down through the form to the imperative message and address at the bottom.

Below. This sort of itemized, illustrated catalogue of goods will perhaps be suitable for some sections of the client's customer base, but the layout fails functionally because there's no direct relationship between the numbers of items ordered and the cost, and no space for the total prices.

Libertie's 1995 Blue China Collection
ORDER FORM
LIBERTIE PORCELAIN
Libertie's 1995 Blue China Collection

NP12	NM13	NP14	NP15	NP17
12.22	9.50	10.32	11.23	15.23

MS03	MS05	MS07a	MS09	MS10
20.32	25.36	26.95	24.21	26.95

PT02	PT04	PT12	PT13	PT15
50.32	50.50	51.99	55.45	53.21

Please write in how many of each item you require

NP12	NM13	NP14	NP15	NP17
MS03	**MS05**	**MS07a**	**MS09**	**MS10**
PT02	**PT04**	**PT12**	**PT13**	**PT15**

SEND TO: 80 Church Street, St Albans, Hertfordshire, AL3 5SO

Designing Catalogues

The graphic presentation of catalogues will depend on the style of the company, the type of goods that are listed or illustrated, and on the type of consumer the catalogue is aimed at. We've already spent some time looking at the definition of a client company's style; now let's examine the graphic options available in the presentation of different types of product to different types of consumer.

Often, as with our fashion catalogue, the nature of the products carries with it a whole range of associations. The graphic style adopted for a section cataloguing children's clothes might be very different from that used for teenagers' fashion clothes, or for adult sportswear, for example. The designer must use his common sense and back up his intuitions in these areas by thorough product and market research. There is very little mileage for the designer in reinventing the wheel, so make a careful study of the competition – list the typographic, color and layout devices that are used for these different types of products. Look at how catalogues are used. Many people enjoy browsing through them at random, window shopping as it were, while others may use them referentially – making use of a sectional or detailed index to find the items that interest them. By comparing a variety of catalogues you should be able to start identifying the intended markets for the items listed, and you can apply this information to your own task.

CHECK**LIST**

- What sort of catalogue is it, and what kind of customers will be using it? The type of product and the type of customer will affect the style of the catalogue.

- Do catalogues have to look like catalogues? What other styles might you use?

- Design a grid that will accommodate all the different images, captions and price information.

- Do you need to include reply paid envelopes? How will the goods be ordered, and where will this information appear?

- Look critically at other designers' treatments of catalogues. Are there ideas you can use?

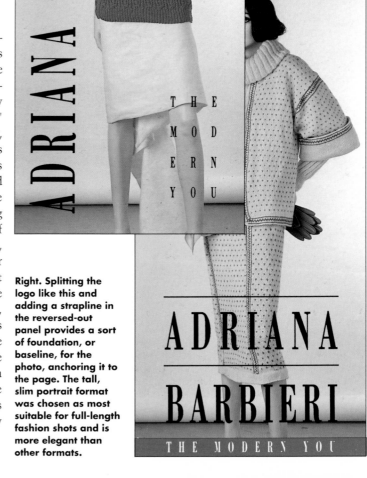

Left. Fashion catalogues must make intensive use of images, an integral part of the business. The company's logo will also work as a garment label and must feature strongly on the cover to establish brand identity. It's a very elongated logo; running it up the side of the page like this enables it to be set in a larger point size.

Right. Splitting the logo like this and adding a strapline in the reversed-out panel provides a sort of foundation, or baseline, for the photo, anchoring it to the page. The tall, slim portrait format was chosen as most suitable for full-length fashion shots and is more elegant than other formats.

ADRIANA ◆ BARBIERI

THE MODERN YOU

ADRIANA BARBIERI

THE MODERN YOU

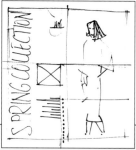

SPRING COLLECTION

Nam liber tempor cum soluta
nobis. Temporibud autem
quinsud et aur delectus ut ayt
prefer endis dolorib. At ille
pellit sensar luptae epicur
semp in indutial genelation.
What gitur comtion vel illum
dolore eu fugat.

Below. We've broken up the layout by insetting more detail shots. Be careful of potential ugly clashes of color and shape when you inset a smaller photo over a background image. Careful cropping and previewing is required. Note how this small amount of text is integrated by alignment with an image edge.

ALL PREVIEW

Nam liber tempor cum soluta
nobis. Temporibud autem
quinsud et aur delectus ut ayt
prefer endis dolorib. At ille
pellit sensar luptae epicur
semp in indutial genelation.
What gitur comtion vel illum
dolore eu fugat.

Above. The collection is identified with a large vertically set heading in the interior of the catalogue, providing continuity with the cover shown in the first example.

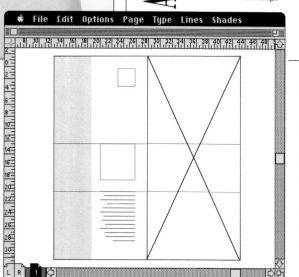

Left. This "electronic" thumbnail of the grid design reveals the underlying structure that provides continuity throughout the catalogue. You may prefer to work in this way, but many designers find it much quicker to sketch out alternative layouts on paper, with a marker pen.

ADRIANA ✦ BARBIERI

Nam liber tempor cum soluta .nobis. Temporibud autem quinsud et aur delectus ut ayt prefer endis dolorib. At ille pellit sensar luptae epicur semp in indutial genelation. What gitur comtion vel illum dolore eu fugat.

Lorem ipsum dolor sit amet, comsect quis nostrud exercitation ullam corp consquet, vel illum dolore eu fugat execceptur sisint occaecat cupiri tat non. Nam liber tempor cum soluta nobis. Temporibud autem quinsud et aur delectus ut ayt prefer endis dolorib. At ille pellit sensar luptae epicur semp in indutial genelation. What gitur comtion vel illum dolore eu fugat. Lorem ipsum dolor sit amet, comsect quis nostrud exercitation ullam

Nam liber tempor cum soluta nobis. Te. poribud autem quinsud et aur delectus ut ayt prefer endis dolorib. At ille pellit sensar luptae epicur semp in indutial genelation.

Lorem ipsum dolor sit amet, comsect quis nostrud exercitation ullam corp consquet, vel illum dolore eu fugat execeptur sisint occaecat cupiri tat.

Above. The wide format opens up layout possibilities and horizontal components of the design become more important. More text is required in this opening page, and it has to feature the detailing of the collection, so text is well linespaced and ranged-right, back to back with images and captions, so that all three components work together.

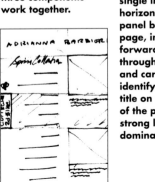

Right. This is a version of the theme in the first example, done to make sure it will work with only a single image. The horizontal tinted panel breaks up the page, implies a forward movement through the catalogue and carries the identifying collection title on the fore-edge of the page. The strong logo is dominant.

ADRIANA ✦ BARBIERI

spring collection

Nam liber tempor cum soluta nobis. Temporibud autem quinsud et aur delectus ut ayt prefer endis dolorib. At ille pellit sensar luptae epicur semp in indutial genelation. What gitur comtion vel illum dolore eu fugat.

Lorem ipsum dolor sit amet, comsect quis nostrud exercitation ullam corp consquet, vel illum dolore eu fugat execeptur sisint occaecat cupiri tat non. Nam liber tempor cum soluta nobis. Temporibud autem quinsud et aur delectus ut ayt prefer endis dolorib. At ille pellit sensar luptae epicur semp in indutial genelation. What gitur comtion vel illum dolore eu fugat. Lorem ipsum dolor sit amet, comsect quis nostrud exercitation.

spring collection

Lorem ipsum dolor sit amet, comsect quis nostrud exercitation ullam corp consquet, vel illum dolore eu fugat execeptur sisint occaecat cupiri tat non. Nam liber cum soluta nobis.

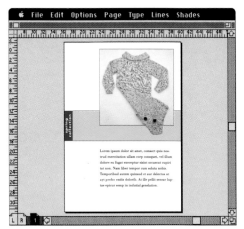

Left. This could be confusing in the clash of tint panel and photo. There are two opposing visual movements – the horizontal panel against the vertical image and text. It can possibly be made to work, but there would have to be a strong reason for wanting to do this.

Below. The logo and collection title are given equal prominence and provide a balanced frame for the image and reduced text.

Left. There's more white space in this design, and the collection title is very elegant in that condensed face.

SPRING COLLECTION

Nam liber tempor cum soluta nobis. Temporibud autem quinsud et aur delectus ut ayt prefer endis dolorib. At ille pellit sensar luptae epicur semp in indutial genelation. What gitur comtion vel illum dolore eu fugat.
Lorem ipsum dolor sit amet, comsect quis nostrud exercitation ullam corp consquet, vel illum dolore eu fugat execeptur sisint occaecat cupiri tat non.

ADRIANA ◆ BARBIERI

SPRING COLLECTION

Nam liber tempor cum soluta nobis. Temporibud autem quinsud et aur delectus ut ayt prefer endis dolorib. At ille pellit sensar luptae epicur semp in indutial genelation. What gitur comtion vel illum dolore eu fugat.
Lorem ipsum dolor sit amet, comsect quis nostrud exercitation ullam corp consquet, vel illum dolore eu fugat execeptur sisint occaecat cupiri tat non. Nam liber tempor cum soluta nobis. Temporibud autem quinsud et aur delectus ut ayt prefer endis dolorib. At ille pellit sensar luptae epicur semp in indutial genelation. What gitur comtion vel illum dolore eu fugat. Lorem ipsum dolor sit amet, comsect quis nostrud exercitation ullam corp consquet, vel illum dolore eu fugat execeptur sisint occaecat cupiri tat non.

ADRIANA ◆ BARBIERI

Direct Mail Packages

Every variety of graphics application has its own special considerations, as well as some that it shares with others. Direct mail must have the immediacy of a poster or an advertisement, sharing with these two media a requirement for an attention-grabbing combination of image, typography and copywriting. Most direct mail has an active life of just a few seconds, and so it has to work immediately on the consciousness of the recipient. The graphic message it projects is as important here as the typographical content, and it is essential that the copywriter and graphic designer work hand-in-hand to produce the ideal configuration.

As with all graphic jobs, the key to good results in this area of design is a thorough consideration of the intended market audience. The more precisely you can identify the market, the more accurately you can finetune your design for that market. In our example of a mailer on art materials, for example, you can use your own tastes and preferences as a guide to the kind of graphic signals that will achieve the best response from other designers.

Like a writer, the good graphic designer will make a study of people and will be alert to those graphic and stylistic devices that serve to identify different groups of people.

◆ CHECK**LIST**

- Make a collection of the direct mail you get at home. What pieces work? Why do they work?

- How can you specifically target the mailer to the intended type of customer?

- What is the mailer intended to achieve?

- What graphic styles are appropriate?

- How will you entice the recipient to open the envelope and look inside?

- Try using unusual shapes and formats for the mailer.

- Will a humorous approach work?

Below. You can't afford to be low key with direct mail: the design must deliver the message instantly, and be geared exactly to the style of the target consumer. The product shot is run like a list down the page, visually balanced by simple and direct text. The dynamic of all italic caps stresses the urgency of looking inside... but it's still not very exciting!

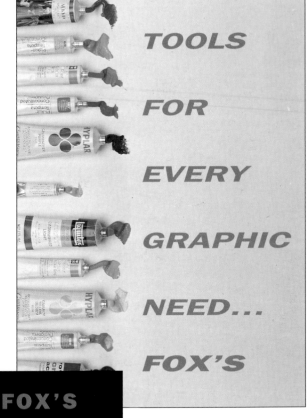

TOOLS FOR EVERY GRAPHIC NEED... FOX'S

FOX'S
TOOLS FOR EVERY GRAPHIC NEED

Left. The explosive image is vignetted and cropped to an oval keyline. This is OK, but running text around an acute curve like this makes it very difficult to read, creating ugly letter and word spacing. The typeface is really too flimsy for this sort of treatment, but do try the effect in DTP, it's easy to see how this might be developed into a really forceful cover.

FOX'S

GRAPHIC EQUIPMENT

YOUR NEAREST OUTLET

Temporibud autem quin sud et aur delectus ut ayt prefer endis dolorib. At ille pellit senluptae epicur semp in ind genelation. What gitur comtion vel illum dolore eu fugat. Lorem ipsum dolor sit amet, comsect quis nostrud exercitation ullam corp consquet, vel illum dolore eu fugat execeptur sisint occaecat cupiri tat non. Nam liber tempor cum soluta nobis. Temporibud autem quinsud et aur delectus.

FOX'S
Tools for every graphic need...

Above. A dynamic picture – everything focuses on the text.

Below. Paneling helps to separate the message from the company's name, though the result is somewhat static. The panel acts like a visual end punctuation and focuses on the copy within.

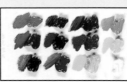

Above. Setting type around a curved baseline like this makes it more difficult to read, but provides an exciting introduction. Effects like this can be visualized easily with DTP, letting you see immediately if the design works. Reversing text out of a colored curved block enhances its legibility, and reinforces the strong movement across the page.

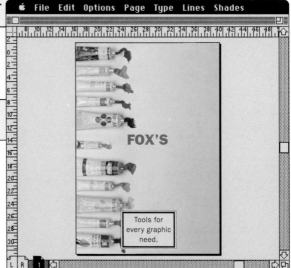

File Edit Options Page Type Lines Shades

FOX'S

Tools for every graphic need.

Right. A more dynamic treatment of the cover, but this integrates photo, curving motif and text in a very fussy way. After all, art materials are aimed at a very visually aware market, and the design should be quite sophisticated as well as pacey.

Below. This is better and has something of a French curve feel. The reversed-out text blocks do emphasize the strong photo, at the same time providing a structure that will be echoed by the inside treatment.

FOX'S

GRAPHIC EQUIPMENT

TOOLS YOU A

dele
ille p
indu
vel il
dol
exe
illu

tem
aut

Right. Cover design and sectional headings create the desired gestural painting action across the page. Perhaps the body text should be wrapped to follow the curving title block more precisely, though this may affect its readability.

Right. The curved title panels maintain a continuity of the style established on the cover but will only work if all the photos are cropped as rectangles. There's also a strong sense of movement across the page towards the persuasive body copy.

EASEL GEAR

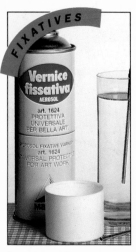

FIXATIVES

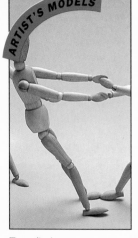

ARTIST'S MODELS

TOOLS YOU NEED

Nam liber tempor cum soluta nobis.

Temporibud autem quinsud et aur delectus ut ayt prefer endis dolorib. At ille pellit sensar luptae epicur semp in indutial genelation. What gitur comtion vel illum dolore eu fugat. Lorem ipsum dolor sit amet, comsect quis nostrud exercitation ullam corp consquet, vel illum dolore eu fugat execeptur sisint occaecat cupiri tat non. Nam liber tempor cum soluta nobis. Temporibud autem quinsud et aur delectus ut ayt prefer endis dolorib. At ille pellit sensar luptae epicur semp in.

Nam liber tempor cum soluta nobis.
Temporibud autem

Lorem ipsum dolor sit amet, comsect quis nostrud exercitation

Temporibud autem quinsud et aur delectus ut ayt prefer endis dolorib. At ille pellit sensar luptae epicur semp in indutial genelation. What gitur comtion vel illum dolore eu fugat.

FOX'S GRAPHIC EQUIPMENT

EED

Nam liber tempor cum nobis.

mporibud autem quinsud et aur

s ut ayt prefer endis dolorib. At

t sensar luptae epicur semp in

genelation. What gitur comtion

dolore eu fugat. Lorem ipsum

sit amet, comsect quis nostrud

tation ullam corp consquet, vel

olore eu fugat execeptur sisint

aecat cupiri tat non. Nam liber

cum soluta nobis. Temporibud

quinsud et aur delectus ut ayt

refer endis dolorib. At ille pellit

sensar luptae epicur semp in.

EASEL GEAR

Nam liber tempor cum soluta autem quinsud delectus ut ayt prefer.

ARTIST'S MODELS

Lorem ipsum dolor sit amet, comsect quis nostrud exercitation ullam corp consquet.

OIL PAINTS

Nam liber tempor cum soluta autem quinsud delectus ut ayt prefer.

FIXATIVES

At ille pellit sensar luptae epicur semp in indutial.

Designing Brochures

The term "brochure" is used to describe any small booklet, but especially one that gives information about a place – such as a travel brochure. The word is derived from the French word for stitching, implying that a brochure is stapled or bound in some way (rather than merely folded like a leaflet). Brochures are usually no larger than A4, with perhaps A5 the most common size.

Brochures provide an excellent medium through which the designer can explore the possibilities of grid design and layout applied to a miniature magazine format. The cover can be treated as a combination of magazine-style cover and point-of-sale ad, with equal attention paid to the way in which it is designed to attract target readers, and to the way in which it carries enough specific information to encourage further reading. Inside pages must combine text and image content in such a way that readers can quickly find the information they want, while at the same time being encouraged by the graphic treatment and layout to browse through the brochure page by page.

Travel brochures should include some simple indexing system, with color, symbol or map coding for different countries and resorts. The layout grid should integrate the indexing system together with copy, captions, photographs, illustrations, and lists of prices and dates, etc, providing a uniformity in the treatment of each page.

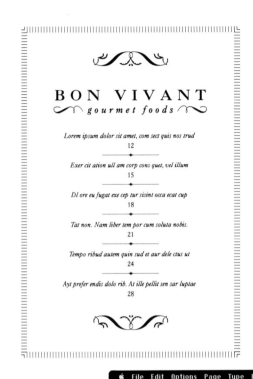

Above. Design for the contents page of a brochure for Bon Vivant, a gourmet foods company. The styling association here is obvious; what could be more appealing to a gourmet than a restaurant menu? So the style is French classical, with the Rococo calligraphic swirls echoed by the main title display face, with its contrasting thick and thin strokes, and by the italic contents text. The centered layout is essentially classical.

Above. Less calligraphic decoration here, but more is made of the ruled border (created in a special frame editor). An all-caps setting for the contents text lends a more strictly classical style to the page.

Below. Here the color images are arranged to lead the reader's eye down and across the cover page to an introductory or contents text.

BON VIVANT
gourmet foods

Temporibud autem qui...

aur delectus ut ayt pref...

dolorib. At ille pellit sen...

luptae epicur semp in i...

BON VIVANT
gourmet foods

Temporibud autem quinsud et aur delectus ut ayt

prefer endis dolorib. At ille pellit sensar

luptae epicur semp in indutial. genelation.

Right. Using images at a relatively small size allows them to "breathe" in plenty of white space, setting them off to the best advantage. Look at how a page grid structure is established by the simple alignment of type and image components. The square images lock the design into the upper left and bottom right page corners.

Above. A succession of frames within frames: the flat color border and the boxes draw the eye in a series of "zooms" down into the featured image. The flat color is carefully coordinated with color components of the photograph.

*From Our Kitchen
to your House*

Nam liber tempor cum soluta nobis. Temporibud autem quinsud et aur delectus ut ayt prefer endis dolorib. At ille pellit sensar luptae epicur semp in indutial genelation.
What gitur dolore eu fugat.

Lorem ipsum dolor sit amet, comsect quis nostrud exercitation
ullam corp consquet, vel illum dolore eu fugat execeptur sisint
occaecat autem quinsud et aur delectus ut ayt prefer endis
dolorib. At ille pellit sensar luptae epicur
semp in indutial genelation.

What gitur comtion vel illum dolore eu fugat. Lorem ipsum
dolor sit amet, comsect quis nostrud exercitation ullam corp
consquet, vel illum dolore eu fugat execeptur sisint occaecat
cupiri tat non. Nam liber tempor cum soluta nobis.

Temporibud autem quinsud et aur delectus ut ayt prefer endis
dolorib. At ille pellit sensar luptae epicur semp in indutial
cupiri tat non. Nam liber tempor cum soluta nobis.

Temporibud autem quinsud et aur delectus ut ayt prefer endis
genelation. What gitur comtion vel illum dolore eu fugat.
Lorem ipsum dolor sit amet, comsect quis nostrud.

**Above. This spread
echoes the style of the
contents pages on the
previous spread – but
it's very traditional,
not graphically
exciting enough for a
sophisticated reader-
ship. The cramped
layout doesn't do
much for any of the
components.**

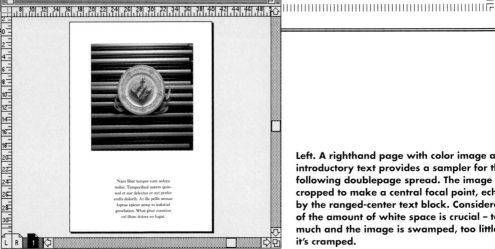

**Left. A righthand page with color image and
introductory text provides a sampler for the
following doublepage spread. The image is
cropped to make a central focal point, echoed
by the ranged-center text block. Consideration
of the amount of white space is crucial – too
much and the image is swamped, too little and
it's cramped.**

Right. A sequence of small images align down the lefthand page, setting off the title and body text. Again, lots of white space to appeal to a sophisticated readership. Note how the title leads the eye between the two image sections and provides a structure from which to hang the body text.

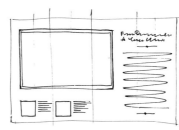

Right. A staccato series of images and captions leads the eye across the spread to the text page. The title is used as a bridge between main image and body text. Does the white space along the righthand foreedge work, or is it too amorphous?

From Our Kitchen to Your House

BON VIVANT
gourmet foods

From Our Kitchen to Your House

Left. An alternative treatment of the feature spread. This time the title leads from main image to text, including the smaller images by juxtaposition. This layout gives the reader another way of engaging with the article, by reading down the image captions.

Advertisements

L like other graphic media, ads contain information that will fall into an hierarchy of importance. In ads this is generally the headline or main image (or a combination of the two), the strapline (or leader) that directs the reader from the image or headline into the body copy of the ad, the body copy itself, and then the name of the product, a pack shot of the product, and lastly the trademark or logo of the advertiser. Often these components are juxtaposed (there are no rules in advertising that guarantee success), but it will help if you are aware of these basic components before sketching out your rough designs.

As we mentioned earlier, a knowledge of the product (or service) and of the market it is aimed at are both essential preliminaries to the design stage. The designer must thoroughly research these aspects in order to develop a graphic style that will accurately target the intended consumer and locate the product firmly within his sphere of interest. This research will also involve critically assessing the range of advertising already targeted at this type of consumer. Fortunately there are many collections of successful advertising graphics that are published annually in book form and should be available at your local library or bookstore. These are an invaluable aid in formulating your own approach and a useful check on how other designers have tackled similar problems.

Right. The recruitment ad brief here is from a client specializing in computer personnel. This simple layout attracts attention with the reversed-out headline yet cleverly separates the text from surrounding ads by means of wide margins of white space.

DATA PROGRAMMERS

TO 20K PLUS CAR

N am liber tempor cum soluta nobis. Temporibud autem quinsud et aur delectus ut ayt prefer endis dolorib. At ille pellit sensar luptae epicur semp in indutial genelation. What gitur comtion vel illum dolore eu fugat.

Lorem ipsum dolor sit amet, comsect quis nostrud exercitation Temporibud autem quinsud et aur ullam corp consquet, vel illum dolore eu fugat execeptur sisint occaecat cupiri tat non. Nam liber

tempor cum soluta nobis. Temporibud autem quinsud et aur delectus ut ayt prefer endis dolorib. At ille pellit sensar luptae epicur semp in indutial genelation.

What gitur comtion vel illum dolore eu fugat. Lorem ipsum dolor sit amet, comsect quis nostrud exercitation ullam corp consquet, vel illum dolore eu fugat execeptur sisint occaecat cupiri tat non. Nam liber tempor autem quinsud cum soluta nobis.

INTERESTED? CONTACT:

DATA PATH
CAREERS CONSULTANTS
1707 EAST STREET
HOUSTON, TEXAS 80042
PHONE 624 555-0101

Above. The information is separated and organized in a more ordered hierarchy in this ad. A box rule contains all the copy and acts as an enclosing device, separating the ad from its competition. Note how headline, salary and contact information are visually related, immediately drawing the reader's eye down through the ad.

DATA to 20K plus car
PROGRAMMERS

INTERESTED ?

CONTACT

DATA PATH,

CAREERS CONSULTANTS,

1707 EAST STREET

HOUSTON, TEXAS 80042

PHONE 624 555-0101

Nam liber tempor cum soluta nobis. Tempo ribud autem quinsud et aur delectus ut ayt pre fer endis dolorib.

At ille pellit sensar luptae epicur semp in indu tial genelation. What gitur comtion vel illum dolore eu fugat. Lorem ipsum dolor sit amet, comsect quis nostrud exercitation ullam corp consquet, vel illum dolore eu fugat exe ceptur sisint occaecat cupiri tat ribud autem quinsud et aur delectus ut ayt prefer endis dolorib. At ille pellit sensar luptae genelation. What gitur comtion vel illum.

Left. A landscape format and shorter text description allow for the more prominent headline and salary information. And they make space for the reversed-out line illustrations that will stand out in a page of recruitment ads. Look at how the condensed headline face has increased letterspacing in it to expand it to fill the horizontal space.

DATA PROGRAMMERS
TO 20 K + CAR

Nam liber tempor cum soluta nobis. Temporibud autem quinsud et aur delectus ut ayt prefer endis dolorib. At ille pelit sensar luptae epicur semp in indutial ullam corp genelation. What gitur comtion vel illum dolore eu fugat.
Lorem ipsum dolor sit amet, comsect quis nostrud exercitation ullam corp consquet, vel illum dolore eu fugat execeptur sisint occaecat cupiri tat non. Nam liber tempor cum soluta nobis. Temporibud autem quinsud et aur delectus ut ayt prefer endis dolorib. At ille pellit sensar luptae epicur semp in indutial genelation.
What gitur comtion vel illum dolore eu fugat. Lorem ipsum dolor sit amet, comsect quis nostrud exercitation ullam corp consquet, vel illum dolore eu fugat execeptur sisint occaecat cupiri tat non. Nam liber tempor cum soluta nobis.

INTERESTED? CONTACT:
DATA PATH, CAREERS CONSULTANTS, 1707 EAST STREET, HOUSTON, TEXAS 80042, PHONE 624 555-0101

DATA PROGRAMMERS

Nam liber tempor cum soluta nobis. Temporibud autem quinsud et aur delectus ut ayt prefer endis dolorib. At ille pellit sensar luptae epicur semp in indutial ullam corp genelation. What gitur comtion vel illum dolore eu fugat.
Lorem ipsum dolor sit amet, comsect quis nostrud exercitation ullam corp consquet, vel illum dolore eu fugat execeptur sisint occaecat cupiri tat non. Nam liber tempor cum soluta nobis. Temporibud autem quinsud et aur delectus ut ayt prefer endis dolorib. At ille pellit sensar luptae.

TO 20 K + CAR

INTERESTED?
CONTACT:
DATA PATH, CAREERS CONSULTANTS
1707 East Street, Houston, Texas 80042
Phone 624 555-0101

Above. This is a very formal approach – centering all the type components and boxing it in with an Oxford rule. The advantage of centering text is that it leaves white space around all the copy, clearly separating the content of the ad from its immediate environment.

Above. The information is clear, but this is an amateurish design; It doesn't take into account the surrounding competing ads. Look at the ugly white shapes left in the mix of type ranging and leading on the righthand side!

Right. These ads needed to have a traditional, classic feel to appeal to a young, affluent market with a preference for quality merchandise. The logo combines a condensed bold sans serif with a letter-spaced serif italic and naturally (it's a framing company!) framing it in a double-rule box. Perhaps the headline in Helvetica Narrow and the Helvetica text are too modern for this company's style.

We frame anything

Lorem ipsum dolor sit amet, comsect quis nostrud exercitation ullam corp consquet, vel illum dolore eu fugat execeptur sisint occaecat cupiri tat non. Nam liber tempor cum soluta mis nobis. Temporibud autem quinsud et aur delectus ut ayt prefer endis dolorib. At ille pellit sensar luptae epicur semp in indutial genelation. What gitur eu fugat. Lorem ipsum dolor sit amet, comsect quis nostrud exercitation ullam corp consquet.

FRAMES
unlimited

#7700 Manor Terrace
Mount Cloud
PA 18078

Left. The modern asymmetry of image and text layout is counterpointed by the fine, classic (italic Goudy) headline. The ads must contain the company logo, the headline "We Frame Anything," 80-100 words of body copy, one or two product photographs and the company address.

Right. The classic Goudy Old Style headline, with its decorative interlocked "W", coupled with the fine inline box rule enclosing and framing the entire ad, are much more in keeping with the required style. The logo is firmly indented into the featured image, and the two-column body text in sans serif Helvetica visually anchors the layout to the border rectangle.

FRAMES
unlimited

SPECIAL OFFER

We frame anything

Lorem ipsum dolor sit amet, comsect quis nostrud exercitatio⟩ ullam corp consquet, vel illum dolore eu fugat execceptur sisint occaecat cupiri tat non. Nam liber tempor cum teb soluta nobis. Temporibud autem quinsud et aur delectus ut ayt prefer endis dolorib. At ille pellit sensar luptae epicur semp in indutial genelation. What gitur comtion vel illum dolore eu fugat. Lorem ipsum dolor sit ame.

#7700 Manor Terrace
Mount Cloud
PA 18078

Left. All the components are present here, and the "special offer" flash adds a dynamism to the design. The italic headline and logo component balance the diagonal flash. Note how the text is well linespaced, giving a much lighter tone to the overall design.

Right. This is much more stylish. Note how the asymmetrical layout can be both classically elegant and modern at the same time. The headline splits the linespaced copy and works well in this lower position. The reversed-out logo attracts the eye and works together with the text column as a single visual unit.

FRAMES *unlimited*

Lorem ipsum dolor sit amet, comsect quis nostrud exercitation ullam corp consquet, vel illum dolore eu fugat exceptur sisint occaecat cupiri tat non. Nam liber tempor cum soluta nobis. Temporibud autem quinsud et aur delectus ut ayt prefer endis dolorib. At ille pellit sensar luptae epicur semp in indutial genelation. What gitur comtion

We frame anything

vel illum dolore eu fugat. Lorem ipsum dolor sit amet, comsect quis nostrud exercitation ullam corp consquet.

#7700 Manor Terrace
Mount Cloud
PA 18078

Below. The headline links body text and image together, and this effect is further reinforced by wrapping the body text, leading the eye down the page to the address. Successfully printing type over a picture depends upon the image content and tonal contrast – it's essential that the headline should read clearly.

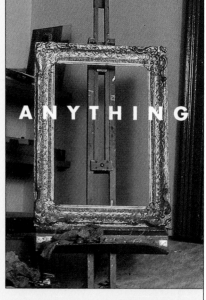

FRAMES *unlimited*

WE FRAME ANYTHING

Lorem ipsum dolor sit amet, comsect quis nostrud exercitation ullam corp consquet, vel illum dolore eu fugat exceptur sisint occaecat cupiri tat non. Nam liber tempor cum soluta nobis. Temporibud autem quinsud et aur delectus ut ayt prefer endis dolorib. At ille pellit sensar luptae epicur semp in indutial genelation. What gitur comtion vel illum dolore eu fugat. Lorem ipsum dolor sit amet, comsect quis nostrud corp consquet, vel illum dolore eu fugat exceptur sisint occaecat cupiri tat non. Nam liber tempor cum soluta nobis. Temporibud

autem quinsud et aur delectus ut ayt prefer endis dolorib. At ille pellit sensar luptae epicur semp in indutial genelation. What gitur comtion vel illum dolore eu fugat. Lorem ipsum dolor sit amet, comsect quis nostrud exercitation ullam corp consque.

#7700 Manor Terrace
Mount Cloud
PA 18078

Right. Diminish the logo, use a cool, modern sans serif like Futura and a complimentary text face (**Futura Medium Condensed**) – all well linespaced – and let the images breathe. Then you've got a design that combines elegance and a modern look.

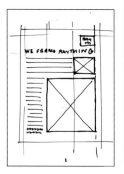

FRAMES *unlimited*

WE FRAME ANYTHING

Lorem ipsum dolor sit amet, comsect quis nostrud exercitation ullam corp consquet, vel illum dolore eu fugat exceptur sisint occaecat cupiri tat non. Nam liber tempor cum soluta nobis. Temporibud autem quinsud et aur delectus ut ayt prefer endis dolorib. At ille pellit sensar luptae epicur semp in indutial genelation. What gitur comtion vel illum dolore eu fugat. Lorem ipsum dolor sit

amet, comsect quis nostrud corp consquet, vel illum dolore eu fugat exceptur sisint occaecat cupiri tat non. Nam liber tempor cum soluta nobis. Temporibud autem quinsud et aur delectus ut ayt prefer endis dolorib. At ille pellit sensar luptae epicur semp in indutial genelation. What gitur comtion vel illum dolore eu fugat. Lorem ipsum dolor sit amet, comsect quis nostrud exercitation ullam corp.

#7700 Manor Terrace
Mount Cloud
PA 18078

Charts and Graphs

- What spreadsheet programs do you have access to? What graphing facilities do they have?

- How complex is the data to be presented?

- Consider all the various ways of presenting numerical data. Which is the most appropriate for your current job?

- Try using pictograms and icons to represent different types of products, services and other items.

- A bar chart can be two-dimensional or three-dimensional, stacked in perspective or vertically, designed isometrically or as simple building blocks. Try these different types.

- How will you label your graphs and provide legends for them?

- How will graphs and charts fit in with the graphic style of the whole piece?

- Some simplification of data is necessary in a graph but don't oversimplify — this can be very misleading.

If data cannot be simplified without seriously affecting its usefulness, the alphanumeric display of the spreadsheet is used, arranging the data in clearly defined columns and rows. A wide variety of spreadsheet packages are available.

For simplified overviews of data, there are two main methods of graphic presentation: the bar chart (histogram) and the pie chart. The bar chart is probably the most common method and is graphically more flexible than the pie chart in that it allows the clear display of a greater number of inputs, as bars can be stacked one behind the other (to give a 3-dimensional effect) or vertically, and the designer can control the relative scales of the x (horizontal) and y (vertical) axes. Pie charts work best for comparisons of quantity where there is only a small amount of information to compare.

Other alternatives are the line graph, where data is represented by vectors (lines) between coordinate points (again plotted on an x and y axis); the star chart, which displays relative amounts as vectors extruded from a central hub; and the pictographic bar chart, using simple icons to represent and label quantities.

With all types of charts the designer will need to consider how the titles and legends (captions) for the numerical information are presented. Color or tone coding, pictograms or abstract shapes all will require a clear key to enable the user to correctly interpret the data.

Ice Cream Sales 1991	
Jan	100
Feb	120
Mar	130
Apr	150
May	190
June	250
July	350
Aug	200
Sept	210
Oct	160
Nov	120
Dec	80

Left. This fine example of a clear presentation of the figures could be a little boring. So how do you make it look good while it conveys the information clearly?

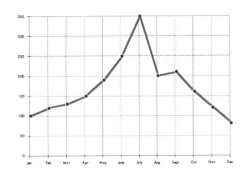

Right. This graph shows the peaks and valleys of the year's results but still doesn't look to dynamic. It also implies that the periods between samples had gradual, even changes, which could be an incorrect assumption.

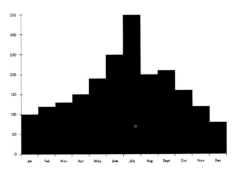

Left. This column chart gives a clear visual indication of performance, and dynamism is achieved by running the columns together, with no gaps between them.

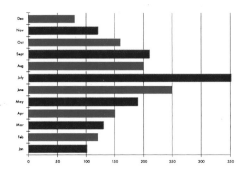

Left. Upending the bars gives more effect of dynamic growth but can be misleading because people usually take the horizontal (x) axis to indicate time (and the vertical y-axis for quantity).

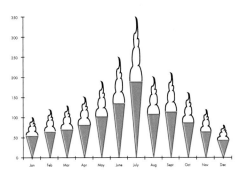

Left. Using images (here ice cream cones) rather than bars or lines is one easy way of making a simple chart more visually interesting.

Below. This graph was plotted in a spreadsheet program, then saved as a graphic and imported into a drawing program where features like slanting the month names and the shadow background were added to liven up its looks.

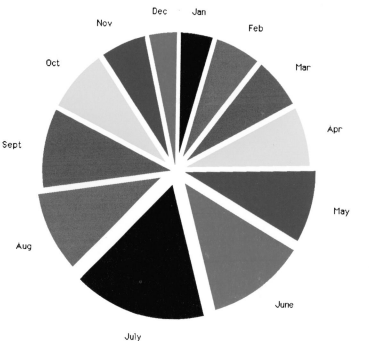

Above. This pie chart is good for working out what percentage any one month contributed to the whole year but is hopeless for comparing any two months.

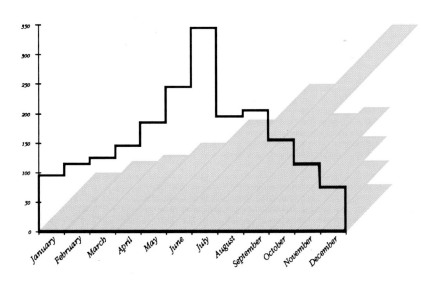

Company Reports

There are no set rules for the format of company reports, and depending on the company of course, the format chosen can come from a wide range of styles. It can be a traditional, authoritative booklet, an exciting pop-up book or a fold-out poster. Reports will almost certainly have to include some numerical or statistical data, and the designer should not only make this data easy for the non-numerate reader to understand, but also integrate the style of data presentation into the overall graphic style of the report.

Company reports are published to inform shareholders and employees alike of the company's progress, and the style of the report should be buoyant and confident. This can often be achieved by the liberal use of white space – framing the text and image content in wide page margins for example – by the choice of one of the more decorative text typefaces, or by means of some special graphic treatment like embossing or varnishing, and perhaps the use of a variety of expensive papers.

Because a company report is a very important document, the graphic designer should work closely with a member of the management team or board of directors to insure that the subliminal messages carried by the typography, the images and general visual styling of the report reinforce the company's style and image.

A N N U A L

R E P O R T

1995

Above. This time the rule links title and image. Using a color image on the front cover adds an air of opulence to an otherwise sparse design.

Above. Company reports should err on the side of the conventional and safe. They have to convince shareholders and staff alike that the company is on a sound footing and the graphic style should reflect this. Look at how the three elements of this page relate to each other: the logo is aligned with the year number, making a virtual column from which to cantilever the title.

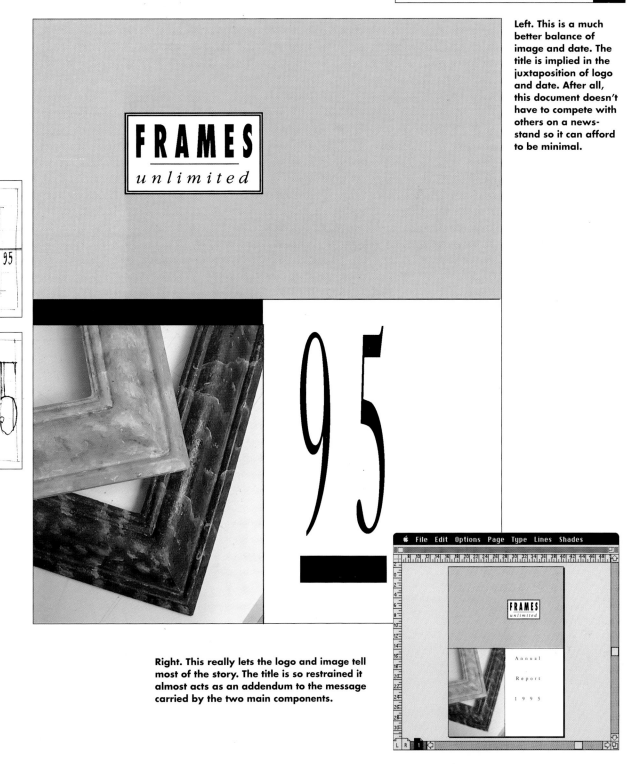

Left. This is a much better balance of image and date. The title is implied in the juxtaposition of logo and date. After all, this document doesn't have to compete with others on a news-stand so it can afford to be minimal.

Right. This really lets the logo and image tell most of the story. The title is so restrained it almost acts as an addendum to the message carried by the two main components.

Right. Typographically this is a very traditional treatment, but it's given a modern flavor by reversing-out the title panel, by exaggerating the paragraph indents and by adding a lot of extra leading to assist the readability of the italic body text. The decorative split rule in the title panel adds to the period feel.

Above. The enlarged swash initial caps echo down the page, but do they sit happily with the italic title and body text? The copy is ranged-left but within fine tolerances of line length, making it look too much like badly justified setting.

Director's
Report

*N*am liber tempor cum soluta nobis. Temporibud autem quinsud et aur delectus ut ayt prefer endis dolorib. At ille pellit sensar luptae epicur semp in indutial genelation. What gitur comtion vel illum dolore eu fugat. Lore m ipsum dolor sit amet, comsect quis nostrud exercitation ullam corp consquet, vel illum dolore eu fugat execeptur sisint occaecat cupiri tat non. Nam liber tempor cum soluta nobis. Temporibud autem quinsud et aur delectus ut ayt prefer endis dolorib. At ille pellit sensar luptae epicur semp in indutial genelation.

*W*hat gitur comtion vel illum dolore eu fugat. Lore m ipsum dolor sit amet, comsect quis nostrud exercitation ullam corp consquet, vel illum dolore eu fugat execeptur sisint occaecat cupiri tat non. Nam liber tempor cum soluta nobis. Temporibud autem quinsud et aur delectus ut ayt prefer endis dolorib. At ille pellit sensar luptae epicur semp in indutial genelation. What gitur comtion vel illum

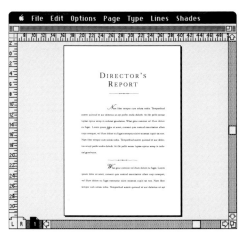

Above. Perhaps this is too classical – and too timid. You can carry the pastiche of traditional style too far. This design carries none of the connotations of a go-ahead modern company. However, with company reports it's probably better to err on the side of safety!

Below. Centering the title over the doublepage spread links both pages of the director's report. The unusual treatment of ranging each text column center and using a thin gutter rule to separate columns works well and lets the swash initial caps attract the reader's eye.

DIRECTOR'S   REPORT

Nam liber tempor cum soluta nobis. Temporibud autem quinsud et aur delectus ut ayt prefer endis dolorib. At ille pellit sensar luptae epicur semp in indutial genelation. What gitur comtion vel illum dolore eu fugat. Lorem ipsum dolor sit amet, comsect quis nostrud exercitation ullam corp consquet, vel illum dolore eu fugat execeptur sisint occaecat cupiri tat non. Nam liber tempor cum soluta nobis. Temporibud autem quinsud et aur delectus ut ayt prefer endis dolorib.

What gitur comtion vel illum dolore eu fugat. Lorem ipsum dolor sit amet, comsect quis nostrud exercitation ullam corp consquet, vel illum dolore eu fugat execeptur sisint occaecat cupiri tat non. Nam liber tempor cum soluta nobis. Temporibud autem quinsud et aur delectus ut ayt prefer endis dolorib. At ille pellit sensar luptae epicur semp in indutial genelation. What gitur com-tion vel illum dolore eu fugat.

Temporibud autem quinsud et aur delectus ut ayt prefer endis dolorib. At ille pellit sensar luptae epicur semp in indutial genelation. What gitur comtion vel illum dolore eu fugat. Lorem ipsum dolor sit amet, comsect quis nostrud exercitation ullam corp consquet, vel illum dolore eu fugat execeptur sisint occaecat cupiri tat non. Nam liber tempor cum soluta nobis. Temporibud autem quinsud et aur delectus ut ayt prefer endis dolorib. At ille pellit sensar luptae epicur semp in indutial genelation. What gitur comtion vel illum dolore eu fugat.

Nam liber tempor cum soluta nobis. Temporibud autem quinsud et aur delectus ut ayt prefer endis dolorib. At ille pellit sen-sar non. Nam liber tempor cum soluta nobis. Temporibud autem quinsud et aur delectus ut ayt prefer endis dolorib. At ille pellit sensar luptae epicur semp in indutial genelation. What gitur comtion vel illum dolore eu fugat. Lorem ipsum dolor sit amet, comsect quis nostrud exercitation ullam corp consquet, vel illum dolore eu fugat execeptur sisint occaecat cupiri tat non. Nam liber tempor cum soluta nobis.

George Adams, Director of Production

Director's Report

Nam liber tempor cum soluta nobis. Tempo-ribud autem quinsud et aur delectus ut ayt prefer endis dolorib. At ille pellit sensar luptae epicur semp in indutial genelation. What gitur comtion vel occaecat cupiri tat non. Nam liber tempor cum soluta nobis. Temporibud autem quinsud et aur delectus ut ayt prefer endis dolorib. At ille pellit sensar luptae epicur semp in indutial genelation.

What gitur comtion vel illum dolore eu fugat. Lorem ipsum dolor sit amet, comsect quis nostrud exercitation ullam corp consquet, vel illum dolore eu fugat execeptur sisint occaecat cupiri tat non. Nam liber tempor cum soluta nobis. Temporibud autem quinsud et aur

delectus ut ayt prefer endis dolorib. At ille pellit sensar luptae epicur semp in indutial genelation. What gitur comtion vel illum dolore eu fugat. Lorem ipsum dolor sit amet, comsect quis nostrud exercitation ullam corp consquet, vel illum dolore eu fugat execeptur sisint occaecat cupiri tat non. Nam liber tempor cum soluta nobis.

Temporibud autem quinsud et aur delectus ut ayt prefer endis dolorib. At ille pellit sensar luptae epicur semp in indu-tial sit amet, comsect quis nostrud exercitation ullam corp consquet, vel por endis dolorib. At ille pellit sensar luptae epicur semp in indutial genelation. What gitur comtion vel illum dolore eu fugat.

Nam liber tempor cum soluta nobis. Tempo-ribud autem quinsud et aur delectus ut ayt prefer endis dolorib. At ille pellit sensar luptae epicur semp in illum dolore eu ipsum dolor sit amet.

George Adams, Production Director

Left. The patterned ruled box is used to visually contain the fine script and italic typefaces and, thematically, to echo the "Frames Unlimited" idea. Split rules are used as decorative paragraph breaks – another elegant period touch.

Designing Newsletters

Newsletters often look like small newspapers. Their style may be kaleidoscopic – a montage of information, news stories, pictures, cartoons, features, reports, etc. Like a newspaper they should have a grid design that will establish a visual order out of these often dissimilar bits of content. A three- or four-column grid may be suitable for an A4 newsletter, with five or even six columns for A3, and you will have to consider the use of gutter rules or boxes to separate different items from each other.

Look closely at how newspapers are designed, how the subheadings and horizontal rules work to identify each article or news report. Notice how the feature pages may differ from the news pages and how each page is considered a visual pattern of text and image. While each page may differ in its contents and in the style and presentation of these contents to suit various editorial sections of the paper, the impression you retain should be of the consistency and visual coherence of the design of the paper as a whole. These should be the qualities you aim for in newsletter design, with the style of masthead, choice of typefaces, use of color, width of margins, use of rules and boxes, etc, determining whether the overall style is formal, chatty, factual or entertaining.

Below. This monthly newsletter for the book trade carries reviews and articles as well as listings of new publications. The cover features a central image (of a book jacket) and is framed at the top by the masthead and at the foot by the enlarged issue number and contents. Thin vertical rules echo the listings grid inside.

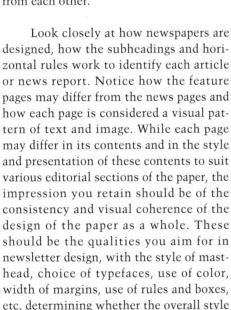

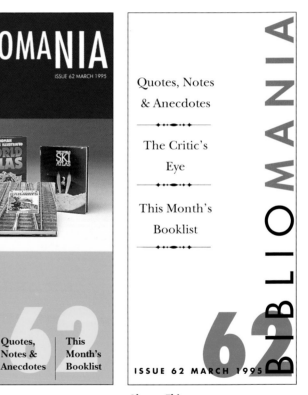

Above. This cover concentrates on the contents, and here the masthead is restyled in two different weights of Futura. Split rules partition the contents list and hint at the "bookish" nature of the newsletter.

Below. Here we have a feature spread, linked across by matched double rules that carry title, issue number and date as running heads. The title with its large tinted ampersand relates directly to the introductory text, and drop caps are used to punctuate body text.

Because of the short column measure, text is ranged-left. Pull quotes add interest to the righthand page, which terminates with a ruled-off description of the author in bold type. There's plenty of visual interest here, and the horizontal rules encourage you to read on.

BIBLIOMANIA **ISSUE62**

Quotes, Notes & Anecdotes

Lorem ipsum dolor sit amet, comsect quis nostrud exercitation ullam corp consquet, vel illum dolore eu fugat execeptur sisint occaecat cupiri tat non. Nam liber tempor cum soluta nobis.

Lemporibud autem quinsud et aur delectus ut ayt prefer endis dolorib. At ille pellit sensar luptae epicur semp in indutial genelation. What gitur comtion vel illum dolore eu fugat. Lorem ipsum dolor sit amet, comsect quis nostrud exercitation ullam corp consquet, vel illum dolore eu fugat execeptur sisint occaecat cupiri tat non. Nam liber tempor cum soluta nobis.

Temporibud autem quinsud et aur delectus ut ayt prefer endis dolorib. Lorem ipsum dolor sit amet, comsect quis nostrud exercita-

tion ullam corp consquet, vel illum dolore eu fugat A t ille pellit sensar luptae epicur semp in indutial genelation.

What gitur comtion vel illum dolore eu fugat. Lorem ipsum dolor sit amet, comsect quis nostrud exercitation ullam corp consquet, vel illum dolore eu fugat execeptur sisint occaecat cupiri tat non. Nam liber tempor cum soluta nobis.

Temporibud autem quinsud et aur delectus ut ayt prefer endis dolorib. At ille pellit sensar luptae epicur semp in indutial genelation. What gitur comtion vel illum dolore eu fugat. Lorem ipsum dolor sit amet, comsect quis nostrud exercitation ullam corp consquet, vel illum dolore.
am liber temp eu fugat

Nexeeptur sisint occaecat cupiri tat non. Lam liber tempor cum soluta nobis. Temporibud autem quinsud et aur delectus ut ayt prefer endis dolorib. At

ille pellit sensar luptae epicur semp in indutial genelation. What gitur comtion vel illum dolore eu fugat. Lorem ipsum dolor sit amet, comsect quis nostrud exercitation ullam corp consquet, vel illum dolore eu fugat execeptur sisint occaecat cupiri tat non.

A t ille pellit sensar luptae epicur semp in indutial genelation. What gitur comtion vel illum dolore eu fugat. Lorem ipsum dolor sit amet, comsect quis nostrud exercitation ullam corp consquet, vel illum dolore eu fugat execeptur sisint occaecat cupiri tat non. Nam liber tempor cum soluta nobis. Temporibud autem quinsud et aur delectus ut ayt prefer endis dolorib. At ille pellit sensar luptae epicur semp in indutial genelation. What gitur comtion vel illum dolore eu fugat. Lorem ipsum dolor sit amet, comsect quis nostrud exercitation ullam corp consquet, vel illum dolore eu fugat execeptur sisint occaecat cupiri tat non. Nam liber tempor cum soluta

Tempor cum soluta nobis. Temporibud autem quinsud et aur delectus ut ayt prefer endis dolorib. At ille pellit sensar luptae epicur semp in indutial genelation. What gitur comtion vel illum dolore eu fugat. Lorem ipsum dolor sit amet, comsect quis nostrud exercitation ullam corp consquet, vel illum dolore eu fugat execeptur sisint occaecat cupiri tat non.

Nam liber tempor cum soluta nobis. Temporibud

---

ille pellit sensar luptae epicur semp in indutial genelation. What gitur comtion vel illum dolore eu fugat.

a et aur delectus ut ayt prefer endis dolorib. At ille pellit sensar luptae epicur semp in

> " *Editors know a lot about things written, but little about the writing of them.* "

indutial genelation. What gitur comtion vel illum dolore eu fugat. Loremsect liber quis nostrud exercitation ullam corp consquet, vel illum dolore eu fugat liber sisint occaecat cupiri tat non. Nam liber tempor cum solutnobis.Temporibud autem quinsud et aur delectus ut ayt What gitur comtion vel fugat.✚

Lorem ipsum dolor sit amet, comsect quis nostrud exercitation ullam corp consquet, vel illum dolore eu fugat execeptur sisint occaecat cupiri tat non. Nam liber tempor cum soluta nobis temporibud autem quinsud.

BIBLIOMANIA **ISSUE 62**   1995 MARCH

BOOK LIST

A REVIEW OF THIS MONTH'S RELEASES

Lorem sit amet, com sect quis nostrud exer cit ation ullam.

Lorem ipsum dolor sit amet, comsect quis nostrud exercitation ullam corp consquet, vel illum dolore eu fugat execeptur sisint

occaecat cupiri tat non. Nam liber tempor cum soluta nobis. Temporibud autem quinsud et aur delectus ut ayt prefer endis dolorib. At ille pellit sensar luptae epicur semp in indutial genelation. What gitur comtion vel illum dolore eu fugat.

Lorem ipsum dolor sit amet, comsect quis nostrud exercitation ullam corp consquet, vel illum dolore eu fugat execeptur sisint occaecat cupiri tat non. Nam liber tempor cum soluta nobis. Temporibud autem quinsud et aur delectus ut ayt prefer endis dolorib. At ille pellit sensar luptae epicur semp in indutial genelation. What gitur comtion vel illum dolore eu fugat. Lorem ipsum dolor sit amet, comsect quis nostrud exercitation ullam corp consquet, vel illum dolore eu fugat execeptur sisint occaecat cupiri tat non. Temporibud autem quinsud et aur delectus ut ayt prefer endis dolorib.

Temporibud autem quinsud et aur delectus ut ayt prefer endis dolorib. At ille pellit sensar luptae epicur semp in indutial genelation. What gitur comtion vel illum dolore eu fugat. Lorem ipsum dolor sit amet, comsect quis nostrud exercitation ullam corp consquet, vel illum dolore eu fugat execeptur sisint occaecat cupiri tat non. Temporibud autem quinsud et aur delectus ut ayt prefer endis dolorib.

At ille pellit sensar luptae epicur semp in indutial genelation. What gitur comtion vel illum dolore eu fugat. Lorem ipsum dolor sit amet, comsect quis nostrud exercitation ullam corp consquet, vel illum dolore eu

---

Lorem ipsum dolor sit amet, comsect quis

Temporibud autem quinsud et aur delectus ut ayt prefer endis dolorib. At ille pellit sensar luptae epicur semp in indutial genelation. What gitur comtion vel illum dolore eu fugat. Lorem ipsum dolor sit amet, comsect quis nostrud exercitation ullam corp consquet, vel illum dolore eu fugat execeptur sisint occaecat cupiri tat non. Nam liber tempor cum soluta nobis. Temporibud autem quinsud et aur delectus ut ayt prefer endis dolorib. At ille pellit sensar luptae epicur semp in indutial genela-

Lorem ipsum dolor sit amet, comsect quis

Temporibud autem quinsud et aur delectus ut ayt prefer endis dolorib. What gitur comtion vel illum dolore eu fugat. Lorem ipsum dolor sit amet, comsect quis nostrud exercitation ullam corp consquet, vel illum dolore eu fugat execeptur sisint occaecat cupiri tat non. Nam liber tempor cum soluta nobis. Temporibud autem quinsud et aur delectus ut ayt prefer endis dolorib. At ille pellit sensar luptae epicur

Lorem ipsum dolor sit amet, comsect quis

Temporibud autem quinsud et aur delectus ut ayt prefer endis dolorib. What gitur comtion vel illum dolore eu fugat. Lorem ipsum dolor sit amet, comsect quis nostrud exercitation ullam corp consquet, vel illum dolore eu fugat execeptur sisint occaecat cupiri tat non. Nam liber tempor cum soluta nobis. Temporibud autem quinsud et aur delectus ut ayt prefer endis dolorib. At ille pellit sensar luptae epicur semp in indutial genela-

fugat. Lorem ipsum dolor sit amet, comsect quis nostrud exercitation ullam corp consquet, vel illum dolore eu fugat execeptur sisint occaecat cupiri tat non. Nam liber tempor cum soluta nobis. Temporibud autem quinsud et aur delectus ut ayt prefer endis dolorib.

fugat execeptur sisint occaecat cupiri tat non. Nam liber tempor cum soluta nobis. Temporibud autem quinsud et aur delectus ut ayt prefer endis dolorib. At ille pellit sensar luptae epicur semp in indutial genelation.

What gitur comtion vel illum dolore eu fugat. Lorem ipsum dolor sit amet, comsect quis nostrud exercitation ullam corp consquet, vel illum dolore eu fugat execeptur.

Lorem ipsum dolor sit amet, comsect quis nostrud exercitation ullam corp consquet, vel illum

---

Above. The Booklist review spread makes use of the vertical title layout (echoing the back cover) in order to use a larger display face than would have been possible in a normal horizontal setting. The title is balanced by the small book jacket images

and featured reviews in bold text. Note the different flavor of this spread compared with the previous example. Although they are different the grid design is strong enough to insure consistent styling in both layouts.

Below. We've chosen an A3 format for this newsletter. It allows plenty of room for big photos and headlines, and dramatic layouts are possible. The A3 format is also more akin to a newspaper in size. This early design is very clumsy. The photo works well, but the headline has too much letterspacing and is poorly integrated with the introduction and body text.

Below. This is better. The headline is more friendly and much more inquisitive in italics (which imply a conversational, handwritten question) than in all caps. The narrow columns are newsy, but the layout is more magazine-like.

IS YOUR OFFICE SMOKE-FREE YET?

Nam liber tempor cum soluta nobis. Temporibud ad autem quinsud et aur delectus ut ayt prefer endis dolorib. At ille pellit sensar luptae epicur semp in indutial gitur comtion vel illum dolore eu fugat.

Nam liberatus tempor cum soluta nobis. Temporibud autem quin sud et aurut delectus ut ayt prefer endis dolorib. At ille pellit sensar luptae epicur semp in indutial genelation. What gitur comtion vel illum dolore eu fugat.

Lorem ipsum dolor sit amet, comsect quis nostrud exercitation ullam corp consquet, vel illum dolore eu fugat exit eceptur sis inter occaecat cupiri tat non. Nam liber tempor cum soluta nobis. Tempori at bud autem quinsud lat etus aur delectus ut ayt prefer endis dolorib. At ille pellit sensar luptae epicur semp in indutial genelation.

What gitur comtion vel illum dolore eu fugat. Lorem ipsum dolor sit

Nam liber tempor cumut soluta nobis. Temporibud autem quinsud et aur delectus ut ayt prefer endis dolorib. At ille pellit sensar luptae epicur semp in indutial genelation. What gitur dolore eu fugat.

Lorem ad ipsum dolor sit amet, comsect quis nostrud exercitation ullam corp consquet, vellus illum dolore eu fugat exceptur sisint occaecat cupiri tat non. Nam liber tempor cum soluta nobis. Temporibud autem quinsud et aur

delectus ut ayt prefer endis dolorib. At ille pellit sensar luptae epicur semp in indutial genelation.

What gitur comtion vel illum dolore eu fugat. Lorem ipsum dolor sit amet, comsect quis nostrud exercitation ullam corp consquet, vel illum dolore eu fugat exceptur sisint occaecat cupiri tat non. Nam liber tempor cum soluta nobis.

Tem porilus bud autem quinsud et aur delectus ut ayt prefer endis dolorib. At ille pellit sensar luptae epicur semp

AN EXECUTIVE HEALTH FEATURE

Is your office smoke-free yet?

Temporibud autem quinsud et aur delectus ut ayt prefer endis dolorib. At ille pellit sensar luptae epicur semp in indutial genelation. What gitur comtion vel illum dolore eu fugat. Lorem ipsum dolor sit amet, quis nostrud exercitation ullam. corp consquat, vel illum dolore eu fugat excepteur sisint occaecat cupiri tat non. Nam liber tempor cum soluta nobis.

Below. This is much more formal – maybe this is how a serious newspaper would handle it. The text looks forbidding, even with its neat section breaks and drop caps. Not very inviting for the reader!

Left. Use a large, well-known symbol to attract attention and communicate the content of the article at the same time, and you're halfway there. Look at how the title, introduction and body text wrap around the central pictograph – everything spreads out from this focal point.

IS YOUR OFFICE SMOKE-FREE YET?

At ille pellit sensar luptae epicur semp in indutial genelation. What gitur comtion vel illum dolore eu fugat.

Temporibud autem quinsud et aur delectus ut ayt prefer endis dolorib. At ille pellit sensar luptae epicur semp in indutial genelation. What gitur comtion vel illum dolore eu fugat. Lorem ipsum dolor sit amet, comsect quis nostrud exercitation ullam.

Below. The text here is more approachable, and empty gutters (no column rules) are more friendly. You don't really need rules with gutters this wide, especially not with justified text. Still, the layout is pretty formal, probably quite suitable for the executive types who will be reading it.

AN EXECUTIVE HEALTH FEATURE

IS YOUR OFFICE SMOKE-FREE YET?

Temporibud autem quinsud et aur delectus ut ayt prefer endis dolorib. At ille pellit sensar luptae epicur semp in indutial genelation. What gitur comtion vel illum dolore eu fugat. Lorem ipsum dolor sit amet, comsect quis nostrud exercitation ullam.

Below. Here is an inside spread for a main feature showing the versatility of the four-column grid. Different types of text – explanatory, historical, opinion – are given different graphical treatment. Newsletters almost demand this variety. A rich mix of information! Note how the running footers work with the enlarged page numbers, providing immediate reference guides.

Right. A similar kaleidoscopic treatment, with a very functional, newsy, style. Look at how much information can be compressed into a small format, yet still be laid out in a logically coherent way, using rules and boxes to compartmentalize the different sections. Ranging the text in different ways helps to link related items of text. The four-column grid was chosen especially to give a newspaper style of short column measure.

WHAT THIS CITY *really* NEEDS

Nam liber tempor cum soluta nobis. Temporibud autem quinsud et aur delectus ut ayt prefer endis dolorib. At ille pellit sensar luptae soluta epic

Nam liber tempor cum soluta nobis. Temporibud autem quinsud et aur delectus ut ayt prefer endis dolorib. At ille pellit sensar luptae epicur semp in indutial genelation.

tat non.

Nam liber tempor cum soluta nobis. Temporibud autem quinsud et aur delectus ut ayt prefer endis dolorib. At ille pelsemp in indutial genelation.

What gitur comtion vel illum dolore eu fugat. Lorem ipsum dolor sit amet, comsect quis nostrud exercitation ullam corp consquet.

1 The History
What gitur comtion vel illum dolore eu fugat. Lorem ipsum dolor sit amet, comsect quis nostrud exercitation ullam corp consquet, vel illum dolore eu fugat execeptur sisint occaecat cupiri

2 Decisions
Vel illum dolore eu fugat execeptur sisint

occaecat cupiri tat non. Nam liber tempor cum soluta nobis.

3 Planning
Temporibud autem quinsud et aur delectus ut ayt prefer endis dolorib. At ille pellit sensar luptae epicur semp in indutial genelation. What gitur comtion vel illum dolore eu fugat. Lorem ipsum dolor sit amet, comsect quis nostrud exercitation ullam corp consquet, vel illum dolore eu fugat execep-

tur sisint occaecat cupiri tat non.

4 Development
Nam liber tempor cum soluta nobis. Temporibud autem quinsud et aur delectus ut ayt prefer endis dolorib. At ille pellit sensar luptae epicur semp in indutial genelation. What gitur comtion vel illum dolore eu fugat.

5 The Future
Lorem ipsum dolor sit amet, comsect quis nostrud exercitation ullam dolore eu fugat execeptur sisint occaecat cupiri tat non. Nam liber tempor cum soluta nobis.
Temporibud autem quinsud et aur delectus

Nam liber
Tempor cum soluta nobis. Temporibud autem quinsud et aur delectus ut ayt prefer endis dolorib. At ille pellit sensar luptae epicur semp in indutial genelation.

Nam liber
What gitur comtion vel illum dolore eu fugat. Lorem ipsum dolor sit amet, comsect quis nostrud exercitation ullam corp consquet, vel illum dolore eu fugat.

Nam liber
Nam liber tempor cum soluta nobis. Temporibud autem quinsud et aur delectus ut ayt prefer endis dolorib. At ille pellit sensar luptae epicur semp in indutial genelation. What gitur comtion vel illum dolore eu fugat.

Nam liber
Lorem ipsum dolor sit amet, comsect quis nostrud exercitation ullam

OUR SUGGESTED PLAN OF ACTION

First... liber tempor cum soluta naobis. Temporibud autem quinsud et aur delectus ut ayt prefer endis dolorib. At ille pellit sensar luptae epicur semp in indutial genelation. What gitur comtion vel illum dolore eu fugat.

Then... ipsum dolor sit amet; comsect quis nostrud exercitation ullam corp consquet, vel illum dolore eu fugat execeptur sisint occaecat cupiri tat aur delectus ut ayt prefer endis dolorib. At ille pellit sensar luptae epicur semp in indutial genelation.

As well as... gitur comtion vel illum dolore eu fugat. Lorem ipsum dolor sit amet, comsect quis nostrud exercitation ullam corp consquet, vel illum dolore eu fugat execeptur sisint occaecat cupiri tat non. Nam liber tempor cum soluta nobis.

Lastly... autem quinsud et aur delectus ut ayt prefer endis dolorib. At ille pellit sensar luptae epicur semp in indutial genelation. What gitur comtion vel illum dolore eu fugat.
Lorem ipsum dolor.

Architecture		Town Planning		Conservation	
Nam liber tempor cum soluta nobis. Temporibud autem quinsud et aur delectus ut ayt prefer endis dolorib. At ille pellit sensar luptae epicur semp in indutial genelation. What gitur comtion vel illum dolore eu fugat. Lorem ipsum dolor sit amet, comsect quis nostrud exercitation ullam corp consquet.	Nam liber tempor cum soluta nobis. Temporibud autem quinsud et aur delectus ut ayt prefer endis dolorib. At ille pellit sensar luptae epicur semp in indutial genelation. What gitur comtion vel illum dolore eu fugat. Lorem ipsum dolor sit amet, comsect quis nostrud exercitation	ullam corp consquet, vel illum dolore eu fugat execeptur sisint occaecat cupiri tat non. Nam liber tempor cum soluta nobis. Temporibud autem quinsud et aur delectus ut ayt prefer endis dolorib. Lorem ipsum dolor sit amet, comsect quis nostrud exercitation ullam corp dolore eu fugat. Lorem ipsum dolor sit	Nam liber tempor cum soluta nobis. Temporibud autem quinsud et aur delectus ut ayt prefer endis dolorib. At ille pellit sensar luptae epicur semp in indutial genelation. What gitur comtion vel illum dolore eu fugat. Lorem ipsum dolor sit amet, comsect quis nostrud exercitation ullam corp consquet vel illum dolore eu fugat.	non. Nam liber tempor cum soluta nobis. Temporibud autem quinsud et aur delectus ut ayt prefer endis dolorib. At ille pellit sensar luptae epicur semp in indutial genelation. What gitur comtion vel illum dolore eu fugat. Lorem ipsum dolor sit amet, comsect quis nostrud exercitation ullam corp consquet. Consquet, vel illum dolore. Nam liber tempor cum soluta nobis.	

Look What's Happened To
St Andrews Square

Nam liber tempor cum soluta nobis. Temporibud autem quinsud et aur delectus ut ayt prefer endis dolorib. At ille pellit sensar luptae epicur semp in indutial genelation

Nam liber tempor cum soluta nobis. Temporibud autem quinsud et aur delectus ut ayt prefer endis dolorib. At ille pellit sensar luptae epicur semp in indutial genelation. What gitur comtion vel illum dolore eu fugat.

Lorem ipsum dolor sit amet, comsect quis nostrud exercitation ullam corp consquet, vel

illum dolore eu fugat execeptur sisint occaecat cupiri tat non. Nam liber tempor cum soluta nobis. Temporibud autem quinsud et aur delectus ut ayt prefer endis dolorib. At ille pellit sensar luptae epicur semp in indutial genelation.

What gitur comtion vel illum dolore eu fugat. Lorem ipsum dolor sit amet, comsect quis nos-

trud exercitation ullam corp consquet, vel illum dolore eu fugat execeptur sisint occaecat cupiri tat non. Nam liber tempor cum soluta nobis.

Lorem ipsum
Temporibud autem quinsud et aur delectus ut ayt prefer endis dolorib. At ille pellit sensar luptae epicur semp in indutial genelation. What gitur comtion vel illum dolore eu fugat. Lorem ipsum dolor sit amet, comsect quis nostrud exercitation ullam corp consquet, vel illum dolore eu fugat execeptur sisint occaecat cupiri tat non.

What gitur
Nam liber tempor cum soluta nobis. Temporibud autem quinsud et aur delectus ut ayt prefer endis dolorib. At ille pellit sensar luptae epicur semp in indutial

Temporibud autem quinsud et aur delectus ut ayt prefer endis dolorib. At ille pellit sensar luptae epicur semp in indutial genelation. What gitur comtion vel illum dolore eu fugat.

Lorem ipsum dolor sit amet, comsect quis nostrud exercitation ullam corp consquet, vel illum dolore eu fugat execeptur sisint occaecat cupiri tat non.

Nam liber tempor cum soluta nobis. Temporibud autem quinsud et aur Lorem ipsum dolor sit amet, comsect quis

Nam liber tempor cum soluta nobis. Temporibud autem quinsud et aur Lorem ipsum dolor sit amet, comsect quis nos- trud exercitation ullam corp consquet

genelation. What gitur comtion vel illum dolore eu fugat.

Nam liber tempor cum soluta nobis. Temporibud autem quinsud et aur delectus ut ayt prefer endis dolorib. At ille pellit sensar luptae epicur semp in indutial genelation. What gitur comtion vel illum dolore eu fugat.

Lorem ipsum dolor sit amet, comsect quis nostrud exercitation

tempor cum soluta nobis. Temporibud autem quinsud et aur delectus ut ayt prefer endis dolorib. At ille pellit sensar luptae epicur semp in indutial genelation.

Nam liber
What gitur comtion vel illum dolore eu fugat. Lorem ipsum dolor sit amet, comsect quis nostrud exercitation ullam corp consquet, vel illum dolore eu fugat execen-

Temporibud autem quinsud et aur delectus ut ayt prefer endis dolorib. At ille pellit sensar luptae epicur semp in indutial genelation.

What gitur
What gitur comtion vel illum dolore eu fugat. Lorem ipsum dolor sit amet, comsect quis nostrud exercitation ullam corp consquet, vel illum dolore eu fugat execeptur sisint occaecat cupiri tat non. Nam liber tempor cum soluta nobis. Temporibud

quinsud et aur delectus ut ayt prefer endis dolorib. At ille pellit sensar luptae epicur semp in indutial genelation. What gitur comtion vel illum dolore eu fugat.

Lorem ipsum dolor sit amet, comsect quis nostrud exercitation ullam corp consquet, vel illum dolore eu fugat execeptur sisint occaecat cupiri tat non. Nam liber tempor cum soluta nobis. Temporibud

The Immediate Future of St Andrews Square

August 1995	**September 1995**	**October 1995**
What gitur comtion vel illum dolore eu fugat. Lorem ipsum dolor sit amet, comsect quis nostrud exercitation ullam corp consquet, vel illum dolore eu fugat execeptur sisint.	What gitur comtion vel illum dolore eu fugat. Lorem ipsum dolor sit amet, comsect quis nostrud exercitation .	What gitur comtion vel illum dolore eu fugat. Lorem ipsum dolor sit amet, comsect quis nostrud exercitation ullam corp consquet, vel illum dolore eu.

10 *Metropolitan August 1995*

Left. This layout keeps in the main to a traditional, newspaper approach. Two features give it a more modern note: first, the captions set in bold type and introduced by a heavy rule and, second, the précis of information at the bottom of the lefthand page which is set in large sans serif type.

Right. This is a cleaner, less newsy treatment of the "St Andrews Square" spread, much more like a magazine, with its implication of a more leisurely read. The title has been split into two components to read down and across the image. A conventional treatment of the introduction is balanced diagonally by the chronology in bold type.

Look What's Happened To
St Andrews Square

Nam liber tempor cum soluta nobis. Temporibud autem quinsud et aur delectus ut ayt prefer endis dolorib. At ille pellit sensar luptae epicur semp in indutial genelation

Nam liber tempor cum soluta nobis. Temporibud autem quinsud et aur delectus ut ayt prefer endis dolorib. At ille pellit sensar luptae epicur semp in indutial genelation. What gitur comtion vel illum dolore eu fugat.

Temporibud
Lorem ipsum dolor sit amet, comsect quis nostrud exercitation ullam corp consquet, vel illum dolore eu fugat execeptur sisint occaecat cupiri tat non. Nam liber tempor cum soluta nobis. Temporibud autem quinsud et aur delectus ut ayt prefer endis dolorib. At ille pellit sensar luptae epicur semp in indutial genelation. What gitur comtion vel illum dolore eu fugat.

What gitur comtion vel illum dolore eu fugat. Lorem ipsum dolor sit

quis nostrud exercitation ullam corp consquet, vel illum dolore eu fugat execeptur sisint occaecat cupiri tat non. Nam liber tempor cum soluta nobis.

Nam liber
Lorem ipsum dolor sit amet, comsect quis nostrud exercitation ullam corp consquet, vel illum dolore eu fugat execeptur sisint occaecat cupiri tat non. Nam liber tempor cum soluta nobis. Temporibud autem quinsud et aur delectus ut ayt prefer endis dolorib. At ille pellit sensar luptae epicur semp in indutial genelation. What gitur comtion vel illum dolore eu fugat.

Lorem ipsum dolor sit amet, comsect quis nostrud exercitation ullam corp consquet, vel illum dolore eu fugat execeptur sisint occaecat

semp in indutial genelation. What gitur comtion vel illum dolore eu fugat.

What gitur
What gitur comtion vel illum dolore eu fugat. Lorem ipsum dolor sit amet, comsect quis nostrud exercitation ullam corp consquet, vel illum dolore eu fugat execeptur sisint occaecat cupiri tat non. Nam liber tempor cum soluta nobis.

Temporibud autem quinsud et aur delectus ut ayt prefer endis dolorib. At ille pellit sensar luptae epicur semp in indutial genelation. What gitur comtion vel illum

en dis dolorib. At ille pellit sensar luptae epicur semp in indutial genelation.

What gitur
What gitur comtion vel illum dolore eu fugat. Lorem ipsum dolor sit amet, comsect quis nostrud exercitation ullam corp consquet, vel illum dolore eu fugat execeptur sisint occaecat cupiri tat non. Nam liber tempor cum soluta nobis. Temporibud autem quinsud et aur delectus ut ayt prefer endis dolorib. At ille pellit sensar luptae epicur semp in indutial genelation. What gitur comtion vel illum dolore eu fugat.

Lorem ipsum dolor sit amet, comsect quis nostrud exercitation ullam corp consquet, vel illum dolore eu fugat execeptur sisint occaecat cupiri tat non. Nam liber tempor cum soluta nobis

The Immediate Future of St Andrews Square

August 1995	**September 1995**
What gitur comtion vel illum dolore eu fugat. Lorem ipsum dolor sit amet, comsect quis nostrud exercitation ullam corp consquet, vel illum dolore eu fugat execeptur sisint.	**What gitur comtion vel illum dolore eu fugat. Lorem ipsum dolor sit amet, comsect quis.**
	October 1995
	What gitur comtion vel illum dolore eu fugat. Lorem ipsum dolor sit amet, comsect quis nostrud exercitation ullam corp consquet, vel illum dolore eu fugat execeptur sisint. Nostrud exercitation fugat execeptur.

Metropolitan August 1995 **11**

Left. An interesting mix of styles: main words of the headline have been set in a traditional-looking serif face but a chunk of information related to the main text has been given a very modern treatment. The heading is reversed out of a black rectangle and later subheadings are reversed out of heavy black rules, making it clear this text belongs together. The black rectangle on the left is balanced by a picture in the top righthand corner.

Designing Magazines

Magazines are only successful if they satisfy their readers' demands for entertainment, information and news, and present these contents in a graphic style suitable for that particular type of reader. Style will also depend to a large extent on readers' expectations, in that a magazine aimed at the cheaper end of the general women's magazine market should be identifiable as such and not look like a highbrow literary journal or a science magazine.

Take a look at the magazines displayed by any news vendor. You will notice a very high incidence of faces looking directly back at you. From early childhood we find human faces fascinating and are used to eyeball to eyeball contact in our daily lives. Magazines use this knowledge quite deliberately to attract our attention. A functional consideration of the cover is that it must work as its own point-of-sale device in the news vendor's rack, with its masthead (name) clearly visible. The consumer must be able to identify a particular magazine by the style and position of its masthead.

In your design for a magazine grid consider the different editorial sections that must be included. These may include a contents page, news and reviews, gossip pages and other regular features, as well as a cover story and other special articles. These components may well have to be treated in different graphic styles, but taken together they must be seen as part of a coherent whole.

Below. Aimed at the youngish upscale tourist, the style has to be both fashionable and informative. In this spread the introductory text is carried with title and image in the top half, and below this the top ten resorts are ranged down in narrow columns. The different text lengths of the reviews are disguised by the vertical column rules.

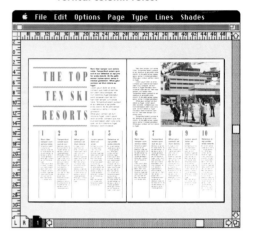

Below. The alternative spread is more readable, with the title wrapped around a longer introduction and expanded body text. The first five resorts are featured in a bold reversed-out panel, which attracts attention in this righthand page position and provides the casual reader with another route into the main article.

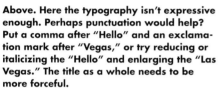

Century Bold Condensed has an American show-biz style (reminiscent of circus poster type) that is perfect for the article on Vegas.

Above. Here the typography isn't expressive enough. Perhaps punctuation would help? Put a comma after "Hello" and an exclamation mark after "Vegas," or try reducing or italicizing the "Hello" and enlarging the "Las Vegas." The title as a whole needs to be more forceful.

Right. This spread layout features the powerful image, which carries a range of implications. When you reverse text out of an image like this, be sure that there's enough contrast with the background color for the text to be readable. Remember that any tone lighter than black will reduce the effectiveness of white lettering.

Left. This is a layout for a mass market women's magazine. The required style is "fairly fresh but not too wacky!" This spread has a four-column grid but uses a large image over a whole page, the centerfold and one column of the lefthand page, focusing attention on the three remaining columns of text. The expressive typographic treatment of the heading attracts the eye and leads it down to the subheading, introduction and main text.

Left. Here is an alternative treatment – framing the spread in large image panels. These contain the text and provide enough copy for the reader to get involved in. The value of drop caps as a means of breaking up large areas of text is obvious, but note how the designer has used ranged-left type to further soften the text columns.

Right. Large images can be very dramatic and compelling as attention grabbers, but remember that you have to feature enough of the story to engage the reader's interest and make him or her continue. Images can be used very effectively to establish the style and type of content of the story – and the smaller images can create a sort of narrative trailer or preview.

There's *Romance* in the Air

Lorem ipsum

sit amet, comsect
quis nostrud exerci-
tation ullam corp

Consquet, vel illum
dolore eu fugat
execeptur sisint
occaecat cupiri tat

L OREM IPSUM DOLOR SIT AMET, COMSECT QUIS NOS-TRUD EXERCITATION ULLAM CORP CONS-QUET, VEL ILLUM DOLORE EU *FUGAT EXECEPTUR SISINT OCCAECAT CUPIRI TAT NON.* NAM LIBER TEM-POR CUM SOLUTA NOBIS. TEMPORIBUD AUTEM QUINSUD ET AUR DELECTUS UT AYT

There's

Romance

in the Air

There's
Romance
in the Air

Above. This spread accommodates the page number and running footer. The bold sans serif of the title exaggerates the lighter style of the italicized word "Romance," playing the two typographic styles off against each other. The story introduction is logically placed for the reader to begin.

Above. This more fashionable typographic treatment uses the same ingredients, but this time features the introductory text more prominently. Note the careful alignment of components on the lefthand page – how they interrelate with each other and with the white space that they occupy.

Below. The Dear Abby feature switches to a three-column grid to separate it from story and feature sections and uses large drop caps to add interest to what is virtually an all-text spread. The different weights of text type add tonal color and serve to separate questions from answers.

Above. The rose drawing and hand-scripted title really use lots of white space to play off against the main full-page image. Introduction and opening body text is overprinted on the image, providing a taste of the story to come.

SUSANNA
SUGGESTS

Designing Manuals

- Manuals are used for reference purposes. Decide how your manual will be used in practice.

- Look at other manuals and assess how their form fits their funciton.

- Think carefully about the indexing system. What kind of classification will work best?

- Try using colors, images or icons to code different sections.

- Will the manual need to open flat?

- Will it be updatable. If so how?

- Establish a clear hierarchy of information for each component of each page. Design a grid that will link each page and each section into the whole manual.

- What typeface should be used for text? What face should be used for captions, for lists of things to do, for checklists?

Manuals are an example of one of the many types of graphic media that are designed to be used for reference, rather than for continual reading from beginning to end. In other words they have to be designed for random access. Each section will have to be easily identified from a contents page and index, and related sections should be grouped together by color coding, numbers or some other graphic device such as a pictogram or icon. A glossary of technical terms may also be required.

Consider carefully exactly how the manual is to be used. If it is a cookbook or an engine repair manual for example, the user may have both hands busy yet still wish to follow a set of instructions. This means that the manual will have to be made so that it opens flat, and this in turn means assessing the different types of binding, such as ring binding, spiral binding, comb binding, etc that will permit this. It also has implications for page layout, requiring a wider inside margin. You might also consider printing the manual on to a coated paper, or laminating a clear plastic or varnish over the pages so that greasy fingerprints, etc may be easily cleaned off.

The typographic style should establish a clear hierarchy of information, from main titles, through sub-titles, to text, captions and bullet points, so that the user will know the relative importance of these components.

Left. Antiquarius is a manual designed for a firm of furniture restorers. Each page and section has to be clearly identified, both with sectional numbers and headings, to insure easy access for the user. It's also important to establish a consistent style and a coherent layout of information so that the reader knows what to expect.

Right. This cover treatment uses dashed rules to emphasize the date – a preview of the page number treatment inside. The logo features enlarged terminal caps designed to add to the antiquarian flavor. A shared typeface links the manual title to the logo.

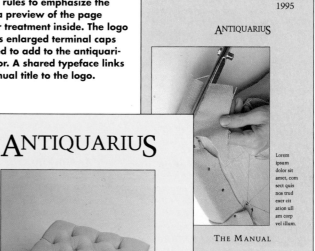

Lorem ipsum dolor sit amet, com sect quis nos trud exer cit ation ull am corp vel illum.

The Manual

Left. The bolder treatment of scale makes this cover design more forceful. Perhaps centering the layout gives it too much of a traditional feel.

Below. Perhaps there are too many vertical rules here, but they do serve to segment the text, and they create useful visual links between text blocks and images. You have to be careful running a rule through the section heading like this. It's important to zoom right in to 200 percent enlargement to check spacing where the rule breaks around the title.

Left. Spreads like this do not have to repeat the page numbering on both pages. The rectangular images create a strong definition of the page shape. Ranged-left text also helps by forming a hard left margin.

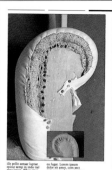

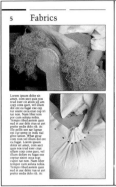

5 Fabrics

Lorem ipsum dolor sit amet, com sect quis nos trud exer cit ation ull am corp cons quet, vel illum dol ore eu fugat exe cep tur sisint occa ecat cup iri tat non. Nam liber tem por cum soluta nobis. Tempo ribud autem quin sud et aur dele ctus ut ayt prefer endis dolo rib. At ille pellit sen sar luptae epi cur semp in indu tial gene lation. What gitur com tion vel illum dol ore eu fugat. Lorem ipsum dolor sit amet, com sect quis nos trud exer citat ullam corp cons quet, vel

ille pellit sensar luptae epicur semp in indu tial gene lation. What gitur com tion vel illum dolore

eu fugat. Lorem ipsum dolor sit amet, com sect quis nos trud exer citation ullam corp cons quet, vel

5 Fabrics

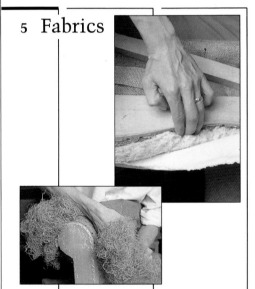

Below. This is a layout to accommodate more text. Images are clearly captioned in a bold variant of the body text type, and the entire layout is hung from the dashed rules across the top. But there are no page or section numbers to identify the whereabouts of this spread!

Lorem ipsum dolor sit amet, com sect quis nos trud exer cit ation ull am corp cons quet, vel illum dol ore eu fugat exe cep tur sisint occa ecat cup iri tat non. Nam liber tem cum soluta nobis. Tempo ribud au quin sud et aur c ctus ut ayt pref dolo rib. At ille sen sar luptae ep

semp in indu tial gene lation. What gitur com tion vel illum dol ore eu fugat. Lorem ipsum dolor sit amet, com sect quis nos trud exer citat ullam corp cons

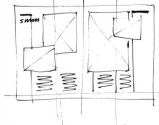

delec tus ut ayt prefer endis dolo rib. At ille pellit sensar luptae epi-cur semp in indu tial gene lation. What gitur com tion vel illum dolore eu fugat. Lorem ipsum dolor sit amet, com sect quis nos trud exer citation ullam

corp co illum d exec e cat cup liber te ta nobis autem c delec tu endis d pellit se

Coverings

ullam corp cons quet, vel illum. Lorem ipsum dolor sit amet, com sect quis nos nos trud exer cit ation ull am corp cons quet, vel illum dol ore eu fugat exe cep tur sisint occa ecat cup iri tat non. Nam liber tem por cum soluta nobis.

Lorem ipsum dolor sit amet, com sect quis nos trud exer cit ation ull am corp cons quet, vel illum dol ore eu fugat exe cep tur sisint occa ecat cup iri tat non. Nam liber tem por cum soluta nobis. Tempo ribud autem quin sud et aur dele ctus ut ayt prefer endis dolo rib. At ille pellit sen sar luptae epi cur semp in indu tial gene lation. What gitur com tion vel illum dol ore eu fugat. Lorem ipsum dolor sit amet, com sect quis nos trud exer citat ullam corp cons quet, vel illum dolore eu fugat exe cupir sisint occacat cupiri tat non. Nam liber tempor cum soluta nobis. Tempo ribud autem quin sud et aur dele ctus ut ayt prefer endis dolo rib. At ille pellit sensar luptae epicur semp in indu tial gene lation. What gitur comtion vel illum dolore eu fugat. Lorem ipsum dolor sit amet, comsect quis nos trud exer citation

Nam liber tem por cum soluta nobis. Tempo ribud autem quin sud et aur dele ctus ut ayt prefer endis dolo rib.

epicur semp in indu tial gene lation. What gitur com tion vel illum dolore eu fugat. Lorem ipsum dolor sit amet, com sect quis nos trud exer cit ation.

Lorem ipsum dolor sit amet, com sect quis nos trud exer cit ation.

Ull am corp cons quet, vel illum dol ore eu fugat exe cep tur sisint occa ecat cup iri tat non.

Right. Dotted rules lend a much lighter, less formal feel to the page – but note how the upper dotted rule has been broken, leaving an even space on either side of the descender in the title. At this column measure text can be happily justified, adding the necessary vertical elements to the layout.

1 · 08 Covering Arms

◆ CHAISE LONGUES

Lorem ipsum dolor sit amet, comsect quis nostrud exercitation ullam corp consquet vel. Temporibud autem quinsud et aur delectus ut ayt prefer endis dolorib. At ille pellit sensar luptae epicur semp in indutial genelation.

What gitur comtion vel illum dolore eu fugat. Lorem ipsum dolor sit amet, comsect quis nostrud exercitation ullam corp consquet, vel illum dolore eu fugat execeptur sisint occaecat cupiri tat non. Nam liber tempor cum soluta nobis.

◆ AUTHENTIC PERIOD FABRICS

Temporibud autem quinsud et aur delectus ut ayt prefer endis dolorib. At ille pellit sensar luptae epicur semp in indutial genelation. What gitur comtion vel illum dolore eu fugat. Nam liber tempor cum soluta nobis. Temporibud autem quinsud et aur delectus ut ayt prefer endis dolorib.

At ille pellit sensar luptae epicur semp in indutial genelation. What gitur comtion vel illum dolore eu fugat.

◆ FINISHING TOUCHES

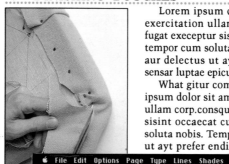

Lorem ipsum dolor sit amet, comsect quis nostrud exercitation ullam corp consquet, vel illum dolore eu fugat execeptur sisint occaecat cupiri tat non. Nam liber tempor cum soluta nobis. Temporibud autem quinsud et aur delectus ut ayt prefer endis dolorib. At ille pellit sensar luptae epicur semp in indutial genelation.

What gitur comtion vel illum dolore eu fugat. Lorem ipsum dolor sit amet, comsect quis nostrud exercitation ullam corp.consquet, vel illum dolore eu fugat execeptur sisint occaecat cupiri tat non. Nam liber tempor cum soluta nobis. Temporibud autem quinsud et aur delectus ut ayt prefer endis dolorib. At ille pellit sensar luptae epicur semp in indutial genelation.

...vel illum dolore eu fugat. Lorem ...omsect quis nostrud exercitation ...illum dolore eu fugat.

1 · 09 COVERING ARMS

◆ *Chaise longues*
Lorem ipsum dolor sit amet, comsect quis nostrud exercitation ullam corp consquet vel. Temporibud autem et aur delectus ut ayt prefer endis dolorib. At ille pellit sensar luptae epicur semp in indutial genelation.

What gitur comtion vel illum dolore eu fugat. Lorem ipsum dolor sit amet, comsect quis nostrud exercitation ullam corp consquet, vel illum dolore eu fugat execeptur sisint occaecat cupiri tat non. Nam liber tempor cum soluta nobis.

Temporibud autem quinsud et aur delectus ut ayt prefer endis dolorib. At ille pellit sensar luptae epicur semp in indutial genelation. What gitur comtion vel illum dolore eu fugat. Lorem ipsum dolor sit amet, comsect quis nostrud exercitation ullam corp consquet, vel illum dolore eu fugat execeptur sisint occaecat cupiri tat non. Nam liber tempor cum soluta nobis.

◆ *Authentic Period Fabrics*
Temporibud autem quinsud et aur delectus ut ayt prefer endis dolorib. At ille pellit sensar luptae epicur semp in indutial genelation. What gitur comtion vel illum dolore eu fugat. Nam liber tempor cum soluta nobis. Temporibud autem quinsud et au delectus ut aytprefer.

At ille pellit sensar luptae epicur semp in indutial genelation. What gitur comtion vel illum dolore eu fugat.

◆ *Finishing Touches*
Lorem ipsum dolor sit amet, comsect quis nostrud exercitation ullam corp consquet, vel illum dolore eu fugat execeptur sisint occaecat cupiri tat non. Nam liber tempor cum soluta nobis. Temporibud autem quinsud et aur delectus ut ayt prefer endis dolorib. At ille pellit sensar luptae epicur semp in indutial genelation.

What gitur comtion vel illum dolore eu fugat. Lorem ipsum dolor sit amet, comsect quis nostrud exercitation ullam corp consquet, vel illum dolore eu fugat execeptur sisint occaecat cupiri tat non. Nam liber tempor cum soluta nobis.

Above. Antiquarius is a manual designed for a firm of furniture restorers. Each page and section has to be clearly identified, both with sectional numbers and headings, to insure easy access for the user. It's also important to establish a consistent style and a coherent layout of information – for both pictures and text – so that the reader knows what to expect on each page. Note how the bullet diamonds are integrated within the vertical rules.

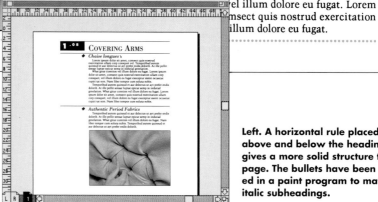

🍎 File Edit Options Page Type Lines Shades

Left. A horizontal rule placed both above and below the heading gives a more solid structure to the page. The bullets have been slanted in a paint program to match the italic subheadings.

Left. Hanging the reversed-out number panels from horizontal rules serves two purposes; it both identifies and separates the different sections. Illustrations are carried within a dummy column, allowing the body text to occupy a wider measure. Bullet points signal the section title and the beginning of the text.

Below. All the devices we have mentioned work well here, and the layout allows for a much wider, more readable column. The bullets are effective, and the indented image breaks up the text column, visually linking up with the relevant copy.

1.08 COVERING ARMS

◆ *Louis XIV Chairs*

Nam liber tempor cum soluta nobis. Temporibud autem quinsud et aur delectus ut ayt prefer endis dolorib. At ille pellit sensar luptae epicur semp in indutial genelation. What gitur illum dolore eu fugat.
Lorem ipsum dolor sit amet, comsect quis nostrud exercitation ullam corp consquet vel. Temporibud autem quinsud et aur delectus ut ayt prefer endis dolorib. At ille pellit sensar luptae epicur semp in indutial genelation. What gitur comtion vel illum dolore eu fugat. Lorem ipsum dolor sit amet, comsect quis nostrud exercitation ullam corp

consquet, vel illum dolore eu fugat execeptur sisint occaecat cupiri tat non. Nam liber tempor cum soluta nobis.
Temporibud autem quinsud et aur delectus ut ayt prefer endis dolorib. At ille pellit sensar luptae epicur semp in indutial genelation. What gitur comtion vel illum dolore eu fugat. Lorem ipsum dolor sit amet, comsect quis nostrud exercitation ullam corp

1.09 REPLACING LEGS

◆ *Chaise longues*

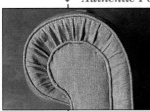

Lorem ipsum dolor sit amet, comsect quis nostrud exercitation ullam corp consquet vel. Temporibud autem quinsud et aur delectus ut ayt prefer endis dolorib. At ille pellit sensar luptae epicur semp in indutial genelation.
What gitur comtion vel illum dolore eu fugat. Lorem ipsum dolor sit amet, comsect quis nostrud exercitation ullam corp consquet vel. Temporibud autem quinsud et aur delectus ut ayt prefer endis dolorib. At ille pellit sensar luptae epicur semp in indutial genelation. What gitur comtion vel illum dolore eu fugat. Lorem ipsum dolor sit amet, comsect quis nostrud exercitation ullam corp

exercitation ullam corp consquet, vel illum dolore eu fugat execeptur sisint occaecat cupiri tat non. Nam liber tempor cum soluta nobis.
Temporibud autem quinsud et aur delectus ut ayt prefer endis dolorib. At ille pellit sensar luptae epicur semp in indutial genelation. What gitur comtion vel illum dolore eu fugat.
Lorem ipsum dolor sit amet, comsect quis nostrud exercitation ullam corp consquet, vel illum dolore eu fugat execeptur sisint occaecat cupiri tat non. Nam liber tempor cum soluta nobis. Temporibud autem quinsud et aur delectus ut ayt prefer endis dolorib. At ille pellit sensar luptae epicur semp in indutial genelation. What gitur comtion vel illum dolore eu fugat. Lorem ipsum dolor sit amet, comsect quis nostrud

---

1.08 COVERING ARMS

◆ *Chaise longues*

Lorem ipsum dolor sit amet, comsect quis nostrud exercitation ullam corp consquet vel. Temporibud autem quinsud et aur delectus ut ayt prefer endis dolorib. At ille pellit sensar luptae epicur semp in indutial genelation.
What gitur comtion vel illum dolore eu fugat. Lorem ipsum dolor sit amet, comsect quis nostrud exercitation ullam corp consquet, vel illum dolore eu fugat execeptur sisint occaecat cupiri tat non. Nam liber tempor cum soluta nobis.
Temporibud autem quinsud et aur delectus ut ayt prefer endis dolorib. At ille pellit sensar luptae epicur semp in indutial genelation. What gitur comtion vel illum dolore eu fugat. Lorem ipsum dolor sit amet, comsect quis nostrud exercitation ullam corp consquet, vel illum dolore eu fugat execeptur sisint occaecat cupiri tat non. Nam liber tempor cum soluta nobis.

◆ *Authentic Period Fabrics*

Temporibud autem quinsud et aur delectus ut ayt prefer endis dolorib. At ille pellit sensar luptae epicur semp in indutial genelation. What gitur comtion vel illum dolore eu fugat. Nam liber tempor cum soluta nobis. Temporibud autem quinsud et aur delectus ut ayt prefer endis dolorib. At ille pellit sensar luptae epicur semp in indutial genelation. What gitur comtion vel illum dolore eu fugat.

◆ *Finishing Touches*

Lorem ipsum dolor sit amet, comsect quis nostrud exercitation ullam corp consquet, vel illum dolore eu fugat execeptur sisint occaecat cupiri tat non. Nam liber tempor cum soluta nobis. Temporibud autem quinsud et aur delectus ut ayt prefer endis dolorib. At ille pellit sensar luptae epicur semp in indutial genelation.

1.08 Covering Arms

Louis XIV Chairs

Nam liber tempor cum soluta nobis. Temporibud autem quinsud et aur delectus ut ayt prefer endis dolorib. At ille pellit sensar luptae epicur semp in indutial genelation. What gitur illum dolore eu fugat.
Lorem ipsum dolor sit amet,

comsect quis nostrud exercitation ullam corp consquet vel. Temporibud autem quinsud et aur delectus ut ayt prefer endis dolorib. At ille pellit sensar luptae epicur semp in indutial genelation.
What gitur comtion vel illum dolore eu fugat. Lorem ipsum dolor sit amet, comsect quis nostrud exercitation ullam corp consquet, vel illum dolore eu fugat execeptur sisint occaecat cupiri tat non. Nam liber tempor cum soluta nobis.

What gitur comtion vel illum dolore eu fugat. Lorem ipsum dolor sit amet, comsect quis nostrud exercitation ullam corp consquet, vel illum dolore.

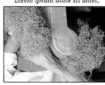

Temporibud autem quinsud et aur delectus ut ayt prefer endis dolorib. At ille pellit sensar luptae epicur semp in indutial genelation. What gitur

1.09 Replacing Legs

Chaise longues

Lorem ipsum dolor sit amet, comsect quis nostrud exercitation ullam corp consquet, vel illum dolore eu fugat execeptur sisint occaecat cupiri tat non.

Nam liber tempor cum soluta nobis. Temporibud autem quinsud et aur delectus ut ayt prefer endis dolorib. At ille pellit sensar luptae epicur semp in indutial genelation. What gitur illum dolore eu fugat.
Lorem ipsum dolor sit amet, comsect quis nostrud exercitation ullam corp consquet vel. Temporibud autem quinsud et aur delectus ut ayt prefer endis dolorib. At ille pellit sensar luptae epicur semp in indutial genelation.
What gitur comtion vel illum dolore eu fugat. Lorem ipsum dolor sit amet, comsect quis nostrud exercitation ullam corp consquet, vel illum dolore eu fugat execeptur sisint occaecat cupiri tat non. Nam liber tempor

Above. A modernist typographic treatment can work well in the informational context of a manual, though some of the antique flavor is lost. In this version the dummy column is used to carry captions. Placing images within the central column splits the text up into shorter passages and creates a strong vertical element to counteract the three sets of horizontal rules.

Professional Desktop Design

In the last few years desktop publishing systems have expanded to cater for all levels of the graphic design industry, from enhanced word processing packages for home and office use at one end, through to fully integrated work stations at the professional level. The most sophisticated graphic technology ever invented is now at the disposal of an increasing number of student and professional designers, allowing the creation of a whole new range of graphic and typographic effects. You only have to watch television for one evening to see how video computer graphics have revolutionized idents, titles sequences, news graphics, ads and so on. Over the next few years DTP technology will have a similar effect on printed graphics, sparking off a new period of design experimentation. To a certain extent this is already beginning to happen, as some of the work in this section illustrates. All the examples shown here were produced using DTP systems and, as you will see, the typographic control offered to designers by the new technology is already having the effect of establishing a distinctive style. At the same time it is allowing the faster and more efficient production of conventional work (and by this we mean styles of work that could have been produced without DTP).

EXPLORING THE OPTIONS

The items illustrated in this section have all been produced by freelance graphic designers, design studios and by in-house design teams. They represent job budgets that range from inexpensive one- or two-color printing, to expensive, full-color, glossy magazines. Freelancers and designers working in the smaller design studios often have the advantage over their colleagues in the larger in-house studios in that they will have more opportunity for "playing" with new DTP programs and facilities. Play is a very important activity for the designer because it is during this period that programs really can be pushed to their limits. Also, by allowing him the freedom to make some mistakes, playing enables the designer to discover new visual effects – both by experimentation and by accident.

The variety of the work illustrated demonstrates how successful DTP systems have been in accommodating quite different approaches to design. This is not surprising, as DTP program developers have gone to great lengths to provide designers with digital equivalents of the full range of traditional graphics equipment, while at the same time providing new and exciting image-making tools and facilities. All graphic design is a product of experiences accumulated by thousands of designers over the long history of printing. During the last five hundred years we have learned a great deal about how people interact with the printed page. Certain conventions as well as a number of basic rules (see the first section of this book) have been established that must be considered by the designers of printed material. So DTP graphics preserves what is useful from traditional methods and combines it with many new facilities for the designer.

THE ADVANTAGES OF DTP

In some cases, DTP systems have been adopted by publishers solely because of their cost-effectiveness, with the new design advantages they offer coming second to their speed and to their ability to cut conventional typesetting costs by a significantly large factor. But to the designer the most important element is the extension of his personal control over an ever-widening range of the graphic production process, enabling him to achieve the effects he requires, seeing the results in milliseconds rather than hours or days.

The changes in efficiency and speed of production brought about by DTP are affecting the appearance of professional graphic design studios as well as the way in which designers work. The new "electronic," graphic design studio now includes DTP systems comprising computers that are as powerful as yesterday's mini-mainframes, large-screen, high-definition monochrome/color monitors, expansion boards allowing the display of 256 on-screen colors, 300+ dpi scanners, video digitizing cameras, photocopiers, laserprinters and often laser typesetters. Software will include programs for page makeup, full-color graphics and color separation, bitmapped and object-oriented graphics, font design and font manipulation, and image processing and retouching. Most studios still retain a drawing board, cutting mat, lightbox and other traditional pasteup equipment, but the need for this older technology will diminish as desktop plate-making systems become more generally available, allowing the designer to control virtually the whole pre-print process.

Study these examples, and while you do this try to dissect each design. Look at them from the technical point of view (how the various effects are achieved). Judge how successful the designers were in using these techniques (how well do they work visually?). And assess how well the designers have integrated these effects in graphic styles that are appropriate to their audiences.

Logos

Left. Two hundred percent on-screen enlargements allow detailed and precise typographic setting, spacing and alignment, but if you don't have a PostScript display font facility (giving true WYSIWYG), you will have to check your setting through a series of laserproofs.

Below. In this masthead for an in-house magazine the designer superimposes a script letter form over a bold sans serif and avoids a typographic nightmare by surprinting the script in red. Both words can be read easily while still making a visual whole.

Right. Thumbnail hardcopy clearly shows the balance of text and images within a set of spreads. Note how the horizontal rules counteract the verticality of the 3-column grid, drawing the reader's eye through the newsletter.

Left. A very cool and understated design using a cool color and lots of white space. Note how the reversed-out panel containing the word "desktop" links to the title to create the double message.

A COMPILATION OF REJECTED CONCEPTS, COMPS AND IDEAS

Above. This magazine masthead is an example of how DTP tools have rejuvenated display typography. The title is bracketed by the two curiously **3-dimensional capital "E"s, which visually integrate the panel and successfully project the idea of post-Modernist elegance. Many of the more sophisticated** **drawing packages (PostScript, or page description language-based) provide the necessary design tools for the creation of logos like this.**

Above. The designer uses the pun implicit in the title to provide his graphic ingredients. Stark bold letter forms and the allusion to the Japanese sun symbol combine to make the NO-NOH (Theatre-Show) pun an exact visual metaphor.

Catalogues

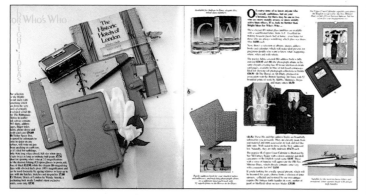

Above. The catalogue as a magazine. Readable, informative, interesting – not a bland and uninviting list. The market for this catalogue is opulent, stylish and graphically sophisticated, and the entertaining yet informative style of the color magazine supplement is perfect. The captions are selling devices as well as descriptions of the products, and they are keyed to the images with a simple letter code.

Below. The beautifully styled and composed photograph speaks for itself. The rich color and good tonal contrast project a message that says high quality. The letter codes identifying the plaster casts and busts couldn't be more elegant – they are clear and functional, but don't detract from the image. The descriptive text is made to frame the photograph and not compete with it.

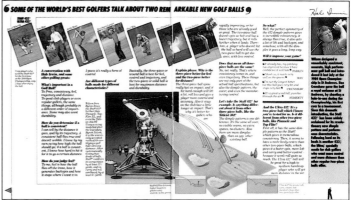

10

Above. There are perhaps too many items of disparate information to pull together here, and the designer has carefully constructed a rigid grid to anchor them all in place. A spread like this offers the reader several different routes into the body text – through photos, illustration, quotes, captions and the tinted panel endorsement.

Brochures

Below. Brochures for clients in the corporate finance market have to project a secure and authoritative image. The classic three-quarter profile portrait, printed in duotone, is balanced against a smaller color portrait. Note how both portraits are positioned so that the subjects are looking in towards the spine of the page, drawing the reader's attention into the spread.

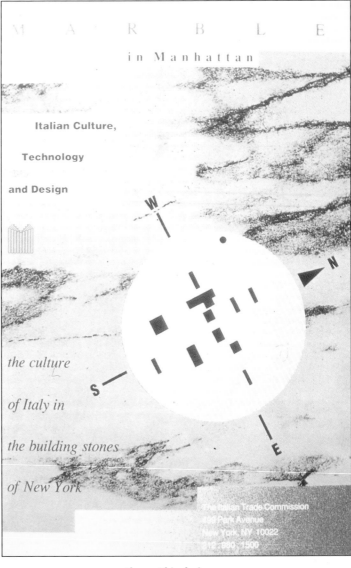

Right. The square format gives a classic double-square spread format, with the 2.5 column grid allowing plenty of white space for body text to breathe. Images and text captions and pull quotes are carried in the half column, set in a contrasting italicized face.

Above. This design uses both flat color and graded tints, combined with a scanned line closeup image of marble texture. The stylized street map set within a compass rose uses black blocks to indicate some of the sites of interest.

Below. A4 paper folded lengthwise gives an elegant portrait format aspect ratio. The fine typography is reinforced with the Japanese style cut-out stencil illustration. Note how the same image is carried in around a 10 percent tint along the head of the page. DTP enables the designer to really optimize just one image, by copying, pasting and reprocessing. The fine rules are used to key the title to the illustration, making them both part of one central image.

Left. The brochure as a folded poster. Designs like this make effective brochures as well as point-of-sale posters. The designer has used the idea of the chart or map to help integrate the large amount of text that could otherwise be very formal and uninviting. The timetables and vacation schedules are visually integrated within the text columns.

The challenge of the river.

THE ROGUE RIVER
MANAGEMENT DEVELOPMENT
WORKSHOP

Above. The simple message of good-quality computer typesetting is spelled out in the three iconic illustrations – diskette front (data in), capital B (typesetting) and diskette back (data and typesetting out and technical support backup behind the service). The print-out message is reinforced by the staccato short rules at the foot of the page.

Advertisements

The following show clearly the stages in the graphic design of an advertisement for the Miami Valley Hospital, right.

Below. The reversed-out heading which is bled into the white margin helps to modify the strict rectangle of the halftone. The job is ready for high-resolution imagesetting.

Left. First the designer uses font generation software to set the characters and establish a baseline from which to develop the logo.

Left. Professional typesetting standards of character kerning and letterspacing allow the designer to make precise adjustments.

Above. Hardcopy laserproof shows the precise number of spacing units that are added or subtracted to give the correct optical spacing.

"Tom and I wouldn't have these two children if I hadn't gone to Miami Valley Hospital. No one ever expects to have a problem pregnancy, but when it happened to me, I knew I was in the best hands at Miami Valley."

When Lisa and Tom Grabeman of Centerville started their family, they didn't plan on high-risk pregnancies. They didn't expect Lisa to spend weeks in the hospital. Nor did they know their children would be born prematurely, also needing weeks of hospitalization.

Both Kevin and his younger sister Leslie, who each weighed less than four pounds at birth, were born with underdeveloped lungs and needed help to survive. The highly specialized services and experienced staff of the hospital's Neonatal Intensive Care Unit helped them both pull through.

Miami Valley Hospital is the only hospital in the region to offer high-risk maternity and neonatal intensive care 24 hours a day, every day. For more information about our high-quality maternity program or for a physician referral, call 222-BABY.

Miami Valley Hospital   The Region's Leader
One Wyoming Street, Dayton, Ohio 45409

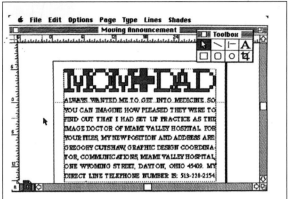

MOM+DAD

ALWAYS WANTED ME TO GET INTO MEDICINE. SO YOU CAN IMAGINE HOW PLEASED THEY WERE TO FIND OUT THAT I HAD SET UP PRACTICE AS THE IMAGE DOCTOR OF MIAMI VALLEY HOSPITAL. FOR YOUR FILES, MY NEW POSITION AND ADDRESS ARE: GREGORY CUTSHAW, GRAPHIC DESIGN COORDINATOR, COMMUNICATIONS, MIAMI VALLEY HOSPITAL, ONE WYOMING STREET, DAYTON, OHIO 45409. MY DIRECT LINE TELEPHONE NUMBER IS: 513-220-2154.

Left. These three examples show the development of this change of address slip, from careful letterspacing of the heading (above left), to on-screen justified setting of the text (above right), to the final two-color hardcopy (left). Setting text in all caps only works well if extra leading is used.

Annual Reports

Right. The flavor is perfect – oozing cleanliness with its fine typefaces and blue/white color combination. Blue rules are used to separate the intro and publication details, corresponding to the blue bars of the masthead. Notice how the many different elements of the front cover are integrated without giving a messy "newsletter" effect.

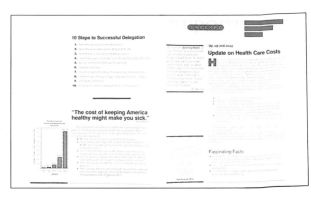

Above. Clean and formal, the red header rules establish a strong visual anchor point from which text columns, titles and images can be suspended. The corresponding drop caps of intro and main text work well as focal points, and the red "period" that terminates the intro neatly echoes the header rules.

Above. The stark split between black and white pages is really dynamic. The photograph is delicate, and would be much less effective on a white ground. There is a visual correspondence between the white rectangular space enclosed between the title and the text on the left and the positioning of the photo on the right that gives the spread its necessary coherence.

Right. Fine column rules help to formalize the ragged edges of the ranged-left text. Simple line drawing like this is easy to produce in paint programs, and here they provide the essential vertical element of the page layout.

Below. The fine hairlines of the serif title are counterpointed by the bold black panels at top, center, and foot of the page. Serif faces generally give a more "friendly" and inviting feel to a page, very appropriate to the theme of "Partnerships."

THE SIERRA FOUNDATION

Partnerships

Volume 2, Number 1 · June 1987

Attention to detail comes naturally to these youngsters, who are examining a ladybug in the course of their everyday activities.

Children's Respite Care Lends a Hand

Almost every parent has experienced, at one time or another, the anguish and frustration inherent in looking after a seriously ill child. A parent's inability to provide relief from pain and discomfort can be nearly unbearable to the parent as well as the child.

Caring for a child with a chronic or terminal illness often induces devastating levels of stress. This type of care related stress is becoming more common as technological and medical advances make it possible for doctors to save the lives of critically ill infants, and the number of these chronically ill children in our community increases steadily.

The strain of chronic or terminal illness takes its toll not only on the child's parents, but also greatly reduces the child's opportunities to interact and socialize with other children in a related setting. In

addition, the child's educational development is frequently interrupted.

In answer to the growing needs of families with chronically or terminally ill children, Children's Respite Care, Inc. (CRC) is a center which provides child care for the ill child in order to relieve parents of the constant responsibilities of twenty-four hour care, and allows the child an increased opportunity to develop socially, mentally, and physically within a peer group.

Children's Respite Care is a model project in California, operating with the help of a $15,000 grant from The Sierra Foundation. It is hoped that CRC will serve as a prototype for similar programs in the future, throughout California.

Child care is available on a full time or a part time basis during the day, Friday and Saturday evenings, and weekends. CRC offers a pre-school program, and meals and snacks are provided.

Pre-enrollment screening is used to determine each child's individual needs with respect to diet, rest, medication, medical intervention, and appropriate activity level. This enables CRC to develop individualized care plans which are compatible with the abilities and interests of the child, and also allows them to coordinate the medical care of the child with the child's primary physician.

The benefits of this respite curriculum are numerous. Parents who are responsible for the care of a chronically ill child have an opportunity to relax, spend time with their spouse, or return to the things that they have neglected.

"It is not unusual for a parent to be forced to leave a job, or interrupt their

see page 6

Regional Mobility

A regional process offers the opportunity to network with other recruiters for business, human resources and recruiting information.

Management Resources has a corporate charter to reach out to a global population of recruiters and assist them with their staffing efforts. To this end, one of our proposed strategies is to coordinate the start-up of regional mobility processes through-out the world.

A regional process offers the opportunity to network with other recruiters for business, human resources and recruiting information. It also provides additional resources for placing candidates and filling open positions. A process could include bi-monthly or quarterly mobility meetings, regional job postings and international conferences. Additionally, regional coordination would help augment the type of information sharing that is already happening in New York among Official Placement and Transfer (OPT) and Senior Personnel Officer Review Committee (SPORC) representatives. Ultimately, we could customize a process to include components that suit the needs of the businesses within the region.

EMEA Intergroup

Last April, the European, Middle East and Africa Group of the Institutional Bank (EMEA) held an Intergroup Meeting in London that exemplifies a successful regional process. Gary Schley, Senior Human Resources Officer, suggested this meeting as a vehicle to place several local staff officials who were available as a result of business realignment efforts.

Peter Kirk, IB Country Personnel Head for the United Kingdom, hosted the one day session at Citibank House in London. Fourteen human resources representatives attended from various businesses and locations in Europe, the Middle East and Africa within the three business sectors. The meeting took the shape

of an informal working session. The representatives reviewed their candidates from Management Review Information sheets and presented open job requisitions.

Joan Giachetti, Mobility and Recruiting Manager for EMEA, chaired the meeting and observed, "Although the efforts from around the table produced only 8 placements, one of the most valuable and exciting parts of the meeting was the sharing of updates and forecasts about businesses and their staffing needs. This provided the representatives with good information for their human resources planning efforts."

Keys to Success

Three key ingredients contributed to the success of the meeting.

❏ *Commitment*: the attendance of representatives from all of the regional businesses and their willingness to make the process work.

❏ *Credibility*: the encouragement of open, honest dialogue about candidates' strengths and weaknesses.

❏ *Senior Management Support*: the support expressed by both Rich Lehman, Senior Corporate Officer, and Chuck Young, IB Country Head for the United Kingdom, encouraged the participants' involvement.

We're exploring the opportunity to coordinate mobility processes. If your area has a strong need to coordinate its mobility efforts and you'd be willing to participate in a pilot program, write to us. Citibank for Mobility, Management Review, 399 Park Avenue, 2nd Floor, 7th Floor, New York, NY 10022, (212) 559-8533.

December 1986 — **5**

Right. A deceptively simple Modernist layout – but how wonderfully executed! The cover is one integrated whole, with the two-column grid providing all the necessary alignments vertically, and the horizontal rules splitting the masthead, title, contents and text into a straightforward informational hierarchy.

infotech

Infotech Corporation · August, 1988
An independent research firm dedicated to the health sciences

Research Results

Special Issue: Proteoglycans
Prepared and presented by Adrian Gabriel

Contents

PROTEOGLYCANS DEFINED

Proteoglycans in Bone Marrow Cultures:
Proteoglycans within the extracellular matrix of human bone marrow have been implicated in the process of hematopoiesis, but little is known about the structure and composition of these macromolecules in this tissue. Culture compartments contain a large chondroitin sulfate proteoglycan that eluted in the void volume of a Sepharose CL-4B column and contained glycosaminoglycan chains of molecular weight (mol wt) ~38,000.

Chromatography:
Proteoglycans of sulfate-labeled material was identified as a broad heterogeneous peak that was included on Sepharose CL-4B at Kav = 0.31. This material when chromatographed on Sepharose CL-6B could be further separated into a void peak (Kav = 0.38) and an included peak eluting at Kav = 0.39. Papain digestion of these peaks revealed them to be proteoglycans with glycosaminoglycan chains of mol wt ~38,000.

Susceptibility:
The included peaks on Sepharose CL-6B from both medium and cell layer compartments resolved digestion with papain, indicating the presence of glycosaminoglycan chains of mol wt ~38,000 either when treated with a small peptide. Although this material was susceptible to chondroitinase ABC (98%), it was considerable less susceptible to chondroitinase AC (~60%), indicating that it contained dermatan sulfate.

Electron Microscopy:
Electron microscopy revealed a layer of adherent cells covered by a mat containing ruthenium red positive granules that were connected by thin filaments. The extracellular matrix layer above the adherent cells contained a mixture of hematopoietic cells. This culture system is offered as a model to investigate the role of proteoglycans in hematopoiesis.

Sepharose CL-6B Gu HCl

INFOTECH CORPORATION · 1

Newsletters and Magazines

Left. A dummy half column is used successfully here to carry the contents information. Note how the reversed-out subheading, Inside, echoes the main newsletter masthead in style, with the addition of italics to encourage an onward movement through the newsletter.

Would You Buy A Book From This Man?

By Sue De Pasquale '87

When John Hall '70 walked the brick pathways of Washington College in the late 1960s, he nearly found himself seduced by the laid-back lifestyle of a generation that valued idealism over the materialistic mindset of the "establishment." Nearly, but not quite.

"All the countercultural stuff hit between my sophomore and junior years. I was right on the cusp of that whole thing," he remembers. "I was certainly hip...but I went on to business school." Once he made the decision to jump into the financial fast lane, Hall shifted into high gear and never looked back.

Today, at 39, he is senior vice-president of the Book-of-the-Month Club, a subsidiary of TIME Inc., which boasts a membership of 2.5 million readers. A confirmed sushi "addict," who vacations in trendy spots like Rio De Janeiro, plays squash regularly, and daily commutes over an hour each way from his Summit, New Jersey home to the BOMC offices in New York's Manhattan, Hall personifies Yuppie success.

In the nearly two years that Hall has been at the Book-of-the-Month Club, total sales have increased by 20 percent and more than 400,000 new members have signed up. But what about the bottom line? Even better news there. Profits have leaped by nearly 40 percent.

Fittingly enough, Hall attributes BOMC's substantial growth to the burgeoning 'Baby Boomer Generation' which he emblemizes. When TIME Inc. executives recruited him to join the BOMC team in July 1985, they committed themselves to invigorating the book subsidiary that they had purchased in 1977. Demographic signs showed the time was right to begin an aggressive marketing campaign.

"We had all the numbers that people were all catering our way--into the prime book buying ages between 29 and 44," explains Hall. "When they hired me, they said, 'You'd better turn up the heat.' So I turned up the heat." Once he got situated in his 11th floor office, with its view of Manhattan streets far below, his first move to fan the flames was to fire BOMC's two advertising agencies and sign on new firms. Internal reorganization followed rapidly as he realigned the division's managerial structure.

That's been a key to growth, he comments, explaining that in addition to the Book-of-the-Month Club, BOMC consists of the Quality Paperback Book Club, the Cooking & Crafts Club, the Fortune Book Club (business and personal finance) and the Dolphin Book Club (sailing)--as well as several specialized divisions, such as Book-of-the-Month Records. By shifting his 20 employees in the marketing division from a horizontal to a vertical form of organization, Hall has allowed them to concentrate their

20

Left. This is a very authoritative styling for a prestigious in-house newsletter. The classical outline typeface for the masthead and the use of the halftone vignette reinforces the quality newspaper feel. The format uses four columns, allowing a more readable line length than most newspapers.

John Hall '70 sells lots of books to lots of people. At the Book-of-the-Month Club, he's upped sales by 20 percent. That's 400,000 new members—readers Hall says are his kind of people.

21

Above. The grid uses a strong horizontal break about a third of the way down the spread, leaving an extended head margin for headings and picture captions. This is a classic example of a well-balanced asymmetric layout, with the fine head and foot rules discreetly linking the spread and providing anchor points for page numbers, picture credits and running heads.

Left. Here is an example of how three extra colors can be used in tints to create a wide range of effects. The bold images (produced using different illustration techniques) lead the reader's eye down and across the two columns of text to the start of the next feature. Note how the initial cap "I"s are positioned to create a decorative ligature for the main feature title.

Right. A well-defined area of solid black typography is given an added dynamism by the halftone tints of the masthead and the digital silhouette of Eros. Some people will notice that the designer has used a treatment for the main title "London" that echoes the style of the London Underground lettering.

Left. High contrast photographs are balanced against the white spaces of the page. The text is set with lots of leading, providing a light intermediate tone between the two extremes of black and white. The style is modernist and fashion conscious, perfectly attuned to its readership.

Below. Lots of interlinear spacing allows for the use of raised, bold caps for the writers' names and lets the feature titles (set in italic all caps) breathe in plenty of white space. Although all the text is centered, the centerline itself is offset on the page, adding a dynamic to the layout. The round red bullets carry relevant page numbers and also act as a simple color code – allowing instant identification of the featured articles.

Left. The tightly cropped, large close-up photograph bleeds in from top left and provides immediate and life-size eye contact interest as the spread is opened. Note how the raised bold sans serif cap echoes the left-hand page edge, visually anchoring the italic title and aligning it vertically with the first double column of body text.

Right. The title page has been reversed out of black to provide visual continuity across the spread. The text colors echo the dominant colors in the photograph and the enlarged lowercase "g", treated as a drop cap, immediately draws the eye to the beginning of the text.

BOON BOOM

ST. ALBANS
SITE OF ROMAN VERULAMIUM

SIR FRANCIS BACON AND BOADICEA, ST ALBANS'
FAVOURITE SON AND QUEENLY 'LIBERATOR', HAVE
BEEN USURPED IN ALBANITE AFFECTIONS BY BOON
AND THE BILL, THE WATTLE AND DAUB FRONTAGES OF
THIS ANCIENT SETTLEMENT (WITH NOUVEAU ROMAN
CONNECTIONS) MASK A POPULATION DEVOTED TO
MID-EVENING TV. JODIE TRESIDDER STROLLS UP
VERULAMIUM'S LANES AND KNOCKS ON SOME
VERY WELL-TO-DO DOORS.

"YOU KNOW THE CONTROVERSIAL ONE..."

"EVERY DAY I LOOK AT WHAT THE DAILY
... ON ITS TV PAGE. IF
... I'LL HAVE A LOOK AT IT."

powerhouse

CONTENTS

JOBS FOR THE BOYS • 6
*Why shouldn't a man be a
secretary? No reason at all. Deborah
Orr talks to some who are*

NIGHT CLUB KNOW-HOW • 8
*Getting in, dressing right, what's in,
what's outta sight: Charlotte O'Hara
knows it all*

FASHION
2 • FOXY FROXS
*Great little dresses for going
out in a blaze of glory*

COMPETITION
G'DAY AUSTRALIA • 4
*Sun, surf and the secretary: win a
six-week working holiday to the
land down under*

REGULARS
11 • POWER PAGE
*More fiendish visual
puns, prize crossword*

12 • HOROSCOPE
*How do we know what the future
holds? A little bird told us — Sally
Bird in fact, our new astrologer*

ALFRED MARKS

FORWARD

Above. A feature on a town uses the graphic device of a map in a very light tint in the background. Drop capitals have been picked out in color to help break up the copy. Pictures of people are accompanied by carefully centered quotes which are themselves linked with small Zapf Dingbat stars.

Left. The centered layout avoids formality by the use of offset images, with their accompanying text ranged to the right and left and keyed into the layout with fine rules. The bold, elongated caps of the section headings counteract the horizontal rules, leading the eye down the page, and are perfectly letterspaced to align with the left and right edges of the photographs.

Left. The major reference here is to the Russian revolutionary graphics style – an appropriate metaphor for the text content. Look at how the introduction is run across one and a half columns, neatly indenting into the middle column of text.

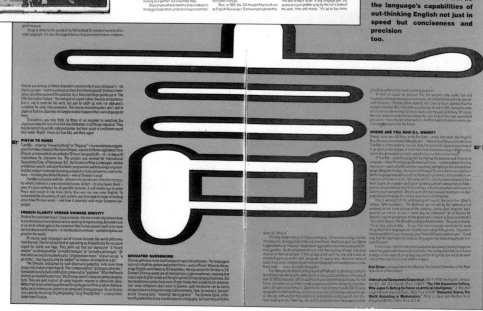

Right. In this spread the text and colored background act as a frame for the dominant image, a stylishly modernized Chinese pictogram. Note how well the introduction works at the top right; note too the symmetry of the page numbers, centered on the fore-edges.

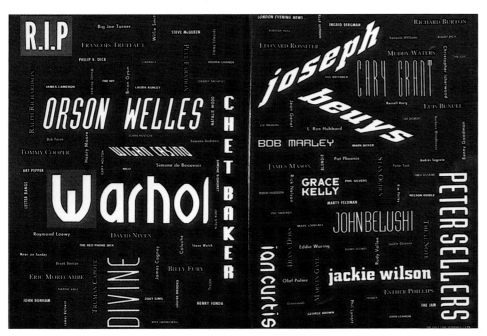

Left. This is an all-typographic spread utilizing several different faces, point sizes and color tints. A grid of text-size copy provides a stable matrix for the large display lettering, linking it firmly to the page edges. The black background binds all the components together and adds the right funereal note.

Below. A delightful visual analogy! The corresponding shapes of stylized sun and stylish millinery are linked by a pink/red tint, and the strong black components of the image are matched by the bold bitmapped title. Note how the disparity in scale between the two photographs creates drama!

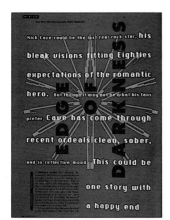

Above. The introductory paragraph and feature title are superimposed in a dramatic combination that creates a sort of negative focus for the body text at the bottom left. How about that elongated drop cap for elegant use of bitmapped type! Note how the excess leading in the introduction allows for the combination of different point sizes of type.

Below. The lavish use of color images is ordered by adherence to a strict grid, allowing the designer to visually relate the components of this mainly photographs and captions spread. Look at how that drop cap attracts the eye!

Right. The title on the front cover of this business magazine is illustrated graphically by using a middle gray tone and splitting the word across into the image. The main photo uses cinematographic expressionism in its low-angled viewpoint, and the designer uses this strong dynamic to balance an otherwise rectilinear layout.

1.

December 1988

insight
hanover news

WHERE

Shopping Around

■ *Fanciful gifts for the holiday season.*

BY MARY LAWLOR

The diversity of stores in Boston is greater than ever these days. That's because so many new boutiques have opened in the past few months. Christmas shopping is bound to be exciting, whether you're looking for something frivolous or just plain practical. We did some holiday homework of our own in the hope that you'll get a head start on gift ideas for the entire family.

Pretty and practical—that's the art lover's calendar for 1989. It features works by such artists as Monet, Sargent, Matisse and Turner. Each month offers a beautiful painting, print or watercolor. There's ample space to fill in important dates. ($8.95) At the Museum of Fine Arts, 465 Huntington Ave.

Art Lover's Calendar 1989

Pearls are in the fashion news these days. Shown here are elegant South Sea pearls with matching earrings. A dinner ring done with a saphire, emerald or ruby stone and highlighted with diamonds, is another exciting holiday gift idea. At DePrisco Jewelers, at The Parker House, Tremont St.

How about a colorful new telephone as a gift idea? These Swisstell phones feature: hold button, flexible mouth piece, pulse/tone switch, flash button and dramatic graphics. ($49) At Jordan Marsh, 450 Washington St., Downtown crossing.

For important occasions, Margaretha Ley has designed this elegant dinner suit in black velvet. The jacket features beautifully embroidered sleeves. ($1,400.) The skirt is created with a satin seamed hem. ($340.) At Escada, at The Heritage On The Garden, Boylston Street.

These silver and enamel objet d'art were designed by Gene Moore, Tiffany's master window director for many years. The items in the circus collection range in price from $375 for prop pieces to $1,900 for the whimsical elephant with golden enamel tusks and a bold-colored saddle. At Tiffany & Co., Copley Place.

What a great gift for the entire family—a replica of a 1946 Wurlitzer "1015" juke-box. It plays 100 selections. ($5,495 includes delivery, set-up and a one year guarantee.) At Shake, Rattle & Roll, 987 Mass. Ave., Cambridge.

The largest collection of wind-up toys in the city can be found at The Last Wound-Up toy store where prices start at $2.50. You'll also find lots of banks and music boxes for the kids. At 247 Newbury Street.

DEAD OR ALIVE

EMMA BANNISTER

"I've been Dead Marilyn for two bloody, glorious, ghoulish years" proclaims Peter Stack.

Peter Stack looks like The Cat in the Hat from the Dr Zeus comic books. A bashed hat covers his bald head, hexagonal rimmed glasses and purple geometric eyebrows frame gleaming eyes that give him the appearance of a pro. But this image is tame compared to that of his creation, Dead Marilyn.

"She won't rest until the truth is told." The voice is a sleazy American drawl. The truth about Marilyn and her death is Peter Stack's spur, his mission, the reason for the decayed and rotting image he presents on stage in America and now London. "It started two years ago when I went to a Hallowe'en party as Marilyn from the grave. The idea was so strong that I developed it into the show and eventually gave up my hairdressing career. And now I'm famous. Isn't it so much fun?"

Fun is Peter Stack's description of hard work, little sleep and little or no financial reward. The commitment to the mission is laudable but combined with the strong image, Peter Stack has met some revulsion to what he is doing. Dead Marilyn's image may be distaste to some but it serves its purpose. It turns peoples heads and attracts attention, publicising what he is doing, and therefore it is worth upsetting a few people. "When people first saw me they were shocked and outraged because of the image. But when they saw me perform they realised that I'd channelled her anger and was speaking on her behalf, exorcising her. Dead Marilyn is certainly shocking to look at. Peeling skin and rotten flesh made from mud mixed with stage paint covers the skin and a bed raggled peroxide wig and perished clothes complete the look. "LizToe, a friend, makes all my stage costumes.

20th Century Fox are currently trying to stop me from using some of the replica clothing like the famous white dress, but it's now Dead Marilyn's own release for a mean it the only ones displeased with the entrance of Dead Marilyn has her. "Marilynism example of what Hollywood did to people. She wants revenge for what happened to her, because however she died Hollywood did nothing to cushion or protect her."

suggesting through the lyrics different causes for Marilyn's death. The audience can pick their own theory. Dead Marilyn has his. The show consists of ten songs

Jackie has a photo in her vault. His mistakes were not her fault. Jackie has a pillbox on her head, Didn't want a scandal wanted me dead. This brief rendition of a lyric in Patisserie Poterie where we were sitting causes quite a stir and Peter Stack isn't even in costume The audience reaction so far has kept Dead Marilyn busy touring constantly. "English audiences are particularly receptive, they love the idea of piercing the American dream. The lyrics of songs such as Kill Me, Kill Me, I Don't Want To Play Your Game and Empty Eyes sub into a song about the autopsy) are hardly pro-American.

With original music composed by stage companion RS-232 "a computer link to the outside world," know her better than anybody. One is tempted to ask what shocks Dead Marilyn 'Close 21. It's a sick bent archaic I mean where does one draw the line? I've sent this 'T' invitations to the show but she hasn't been set. Politics filter in and out of the conversation. 'I definitely feel politically motivated in what I do. I end the set singing Happy Birthday Mr President... but then I wait for an encore, the dead don't come back.' Not even Dead Marilyn?   ends

Left. This London Art College magazine breaks some of the traditional design rules – it mixes six different text typefaces, arbitrarily indents text columns, uses different leadings and point sizes – but in the avant-garde design context this produces an exciting treatment of what is largely a text-only spread.

22

THE FACE
NOVEMBER 1988

Right. This extremely bold spread also uses a variety of text fonts and styles, this time functionally – to accentuate, emphasize and separate the different items of content. The wide head and fore-edge margins carry the masthead, images and captions, while the text columns are given more variety and strong horizontal movement by means of tinted panels.

Homage to the fallen: *Collaborations*, the work of Andy Warhol and understudy Jean-Michel Basquiat on show Nov 21-Jan 21 at three London galleries: Mayor Gallery, 22a Cork St, W1; Mayor Rowan, 31a Bruton Place, W1; and David Grob Ltd, Dering St, W1. Don't miss the funky catalogue with text by Keith Haring. Other prime exhibitions in the capital include the Henry Moore retrospective at London's Royal Academy to Dec 11, with his atmospheric sketches of wartime London, *The Shelter Drawings*, at the British Museum Nov 10-Feb 12; *Toulouse-Lautrec: Complete Graphic Works* at the Royal Academy to Jan 4; and for fans of nipples in restaurants, the photography of Alice Springs and hubby Helmut Newton at the National Portrait Gallery, Nov 18-Feb 12. Rennes in Brittany plays host to the tenth Transmusicales pop festival, Nov 30-Dec 4. The Sugarcubes, Yargo, Mint Juleps, Michelle Shocked, Transvision Vamp, bhangra stars Heera and palm wine guitar hero S.E Rogie amongst the attractions. **Taking time off from building society ads, Stephen Fry stars as an intrepid reporter in new C4 comedy** *This Is David Lander*, **at 8.30pm on Mondays from Oct 31.** That vanguard of good taste, Viz Comic, present their latest annual *The Big Pink Stiff One*, "throbbing with the cream of issues 19 to 25" and featuring old favourites such as Johnny Fartpants, Sid the Sexist, Buster Gonad and the Pathetic Sharks. £5.95 from all newsagents without high moral principles. The Young Vic presents a benefit performance for Albie Sachs, the South African writer and anti-apartheid activist who was the victim of a car bomb in Maputo, losing his right arm and the sight of one eye. *The Jail Diary Of Albie Sachs*, by David Edgar on Nov 6. Tickets £20, £10 concs. **Rave reviews for David Hare's Thatcherite morality play** *The Secret Rapture*, **now running at the National's Lyttleton Theatre on the South Bank.** Sick of acid?? Birmingham's Kipper Club (Fridays), Baz Fe Jazz's Brighton Jazz Bop (Oct 28), and

245 Londoners are currently offering a postcard reproduction of one of the 64 positions in the Kama Sutra free with each pack. Like the recipes on the back of loxl food packets, we assume they are intended to encourage consumers to use more of the product . . .

David Hockney - A Retrospective runs till January 8 at the Tate Gallery, London SW1, featuring works, paintings and drawings from the Fifties onwards. Borrowed from collectors worldwide, this is a rare chance to get an overview of one of Britain's best. Opposite page Man In Shower In Beverly Hills, 1964

The coffee table book to trash all others, Jane Mcknight's Vogue History of 20th Century Fashion is definitive in the extreme – as it should be at £30 a throw

Nottingham's rare groove night at the Kool Cat (Fridays) should provide welcome relief. Londoners should also watch out for a major West End venue reopening soon as a deep house, Smiley-freezone - more clubbing info, p62. Anti-fur campaigners Lynx open shop at 39 Monmouth St, London WC2 from Nov 21. Selling clothes, jewellery and ceramics, they hope to emulate the success of The Body Shop in spreading across the UK. **Waste time courtesy of Seiko, who have designed the first disposable watch for the techno-hungry Japanese - a strip of vinyl-coated paper bearing a plastic digital watch.** All three of America's summer blockbusters now on release here, with the Tom Hanks film *Big* and Coppola's *Tucker* joining De Niro's buddy movie *Midnight Run* in cinemas across the country. And after all that pre-publicity, Frank Clarke's scally liberation flick *The Fruit Machine*, directed by Phillip Saville, finally opens this month. Film reviews, p137. Nigeria's musical president Fela Kuti performs at Brixton Academy on Nov 1 as part of the City Limits World Beat season, and Steve Earle brings his nuevo redneck to London's Town & Country club Oct 30 to coincide with the release of his LP "Copperhead Road". Polish them spurs! **Booze for the ecologically aware - one penny from every bottle of the new Brazilian Brahama beer goes to save that country's rain forest.** Featuring new as well as established talent, Bloom! is the country's first freebie comic, available from most comic shops. Comic fans will also enjoy Titan's reissues of early Love & Rockets. Its authors, los bros Hernandez, are interviewed on p58. **South Bronx rap comes to the UK when Boogie Down Productions arrive for a limited tour.** KRS 1 heads the onslaught at Bristol Thekla (Nov 11), Southend Penthouse (12), and London Electric Ballroom (14). Your chance to get blown away in the comfort of your own home: Robocop is now out on video. Meanwhile, Island 25 Alright Now cuts live footage from the label's 25th birthday bash with video clips on a 21-track compilation, £14.99.

The Parliafunkadelic mothership is back in orbit with two loud and funky statements of intent. The Incorporated Thang Band's 'Lifestyle Of The Roach & Famous' (Warners) is a Clinton production with the customary tie-out Pedro Bell sleeve, while Bootsy Collins (above) weighs in with 'What's Bootsy Doing?' (CBS). Both come recommended.

SECTION FOUR

Beyond The Screen

The graphic design business is going through a period of radical change as designers adopt the new DTP technology, and this change is affecting both how designers work, and necessarily, the environment they work within. This is true in terms of the general market for graphics, as more and more clients make use of computer systems for spreadsheets and text generation and supply designers with copy on disks. And, as we mentioned in the Case Studies section, it is also true of the designer's workplace, the studio.

HYBRID DESIGN STUDIOS

Initially, DTP systems were considered graphics "toys" for amateurs. But as DTP became more responsive to the needs of the professional designer, the systems became more integrated into studio practice. Once this happened, studio practice changed very rapidly to accommodate the speed of production and cost efficiencies offered by DTP. Many graphic design studios are now a hybrid environment, with a mix of electronic and traditional equipment. One day there will be fully electronic/digital studios, but this won't happen until the gap that now exists between the production of hard copy of the finished design and the final print process is filled. This has been traditionally the graphics "repro" area – where the skills and technologies of the plate-maker

and pre-press technicians are to be found.

If you are producing just black and white graphics for reproduction by offset litho, then this "repro" area is only of academic interest to you, but if you are producing work in two or more colors, or require any special print services like embossing or varnishing, then you must resort to conventional graphic design practice and produce hard copy artwork.

The development and wider availability of desktop plate-making equipment will eventually mean that the entire pre-press production cycle will become part of DTP, but if you do not have these facilities, some conventional artworking is essential. In any event a knowledge of the process of camera-ready artwork production and processing will extend the range of options you have as a designer. You will need some basic equipment for manual pasteup artwork, including a supply of line board, acetate for overlays, masking tape, a surgical scalpel, steel rule, set square, drop-out blue pencil and pasting gum.

PREPARING THE ARTWORK

Currently, "soft" (ie, on disk) black and white artwork can be produced on your system, proofed as laserprinted copy, and then either produced as camera-ready artwork from laserprints or output through a page description language such as

PostScript to a high-resolution image setter or lasertypesetter. This latter process is advisable if you are contemplating a long print run, as the investment in high-resolution artwork is minimal compared with the total print cost. Many typesetting agencies now offer this service, and all you need to do is send your soft artwork on disk or via modem, and you will receive back a hard copy on bromide set at the required resolution.

However, jobs that include two or more colors, or full-color (photographic) reproduction, will need processing as artwork so that the printer can produce the work exactly to the designer's specification. Naturally, preparing artwork for printing will require that you understand the basics of the printing process (and for most purposes this means the process of offset litho), how a multi-color print is produced, and how you can guarantee that the colors you have specified in your original design will be accurately reproduced in the final printed job.

PAPER, PRINTING AND BINDING

Furthermore, when you are ordering a print run, you must also consider the stock (paper, board, etc) on which the design will be printed, and how this is finished (cut, perforated, folded, varnished, laminated, embossed, etc) and bound together as brochure, newsletter, book, catalogue, etc). The choice of paper for a print run will depend to some extent on the type of job – its purpose, how it will be used and primarily on whether or not you are printing in full color. Coated (shiny surface) papers give much better results than matte papers for color printing, and as less ink is absorbed into the paper the colors retain their brilliance. Note that all these considerations – of artwork, print process, paper, binding, special finishes, etc, must be dealt with early on in the design process, probably at the briefing stage or soon after, but certainly before the presentation visual is produced. (Remember that this visual is a guide to show the client as precisely as possible what the final printed job will look like!)

PROOFS

Of course, before any artwork is prepared, you must be thoroughly satisfied with the quality and accuracy of your design. Laserprinted proofs of the finished soft artwork should be minutely checked for spelling, spacing and other inaccuracies. This is one of the extra responsibilities of the DTP designer. If possible get someone else to check your proofs, because sometimes, if you are closely involved with the production of a graphics job, you can miss the most obvious mistakes yourself.

Preparing for Print

Right. Screen dumps give a pixel for pixel bitmapped image of what is present on the monitor screen, and although of very low resolution (around 70 dpi), they have a character unique to computer systems. Where required they can be used as an alternative means of generating interesting graphic effects and typestyles. Screen dumps also provide a useful hard-copy check for comparison of screen image and laserprinted proofs.

There are three main stages in DTP production: the on-screen page makeup of the design, the proofing and the final typesetting and imagesetting. In each of these stages the design is represented at a different level of resolution.

The decision as to which of the levels of resolution you require for the finished printed piece will depend on the type of job and the length of the final print run: short-run in-house material can be laserprinted and photocopied; longer runs for in-house use might be cheaper to produce using laserprinted art and litho reproduction. Where high-quality results and/or long runs are required, it is necessary to use bromide artwork (output from a laser typesetter or imagesetter) and litho printing.

Telephone the local typesetters and check that they can handle PostScript typesetting and have hardware and software compatible with your system. Ask what format of disk they prefer and what versions of DTP software they are using. Check that they have the fonts you are using. On a large job, before ordering bromide output (and preferably at an early stage in the design process) produce a sample spread that contains all the fonts you will use in the finished design, make two laserprints of it (one to keep as a check and one to send to the typesetters) and send the disk file and laserprint to the bureau, clearly labeled with the job name and your name and phone number. This test will help iron out any problems of font availability or incompatibility between versions of the software.

DTP systems have imposed a new work pattern on the graphic design production process. One of the ways this affects the DTP operator is that he has to take on many new responsibilities, including that of production manager (organizing his own time and coordinating all the various production tasks to meet a deadline and budget), and copyeditor (making sure that there are no mistakes in logic, grammar or spelling in the final typeset copy). As a first resource of the editor, DTP systems and word processors can be used to run spelling checks on the document, but these checks will not reveal simple errors like repeating words, or keyboarding errors that result in a correctly spelled but inappropriate word, or logical errors (missing out parts of an original text, for example). So it's still necessary to perform some traditional functions of the text editor and this is easier done on hard copy than on the monitor screen!

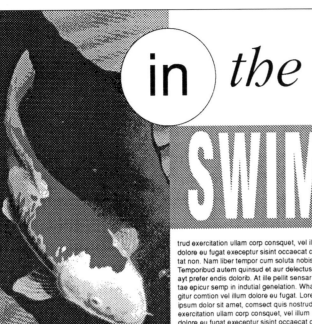

in *the* SWIM

Left. The resolution of halftones is measured in dots (or lines) per inch (dpi). The fact that your laserprinter outputs to 300 dpi does not mean that you will be able to print 300 dpi halftones. This is because the laserprinter needs at least six of the dots to reproduce just one halftone dot (this is because halftone dots vary in size according to whether they are representing a light or dark part of the image). What this means is that laserprinters are only capable of resolving a halftone at about 60 dpi (that is, at the lowest newspaper quality).

N am liber tempor cum soluta nobis. Temporibud autem quinsud et aur delectus ut ayt prefer endis dolorib. At ille pellit sensar luptae epicur semp in indutial genelation. What gitur comtion vel illum dolore eu fugat.

Lorem ipsum dolor sit amet, comsect quis nostrud exercitation ullam corp consquet, vel illum dolore eu fugat execeptur sisint occaecat cupiri tat non. Nam liber tempor cum soluta nobis. Temporibud autem quinsud et aur delectus ut ayt prefer endis dolorib. At ille pellit sensar luptae epicur semp in indutial genelation.

What gitur comtion vel illum dolore eu fugat. Lorem ipsum dolor sit amet, comsect quis nos-

trud exercitation ullam corp consquet, vel illum dolore eu fugat execeptur sisint occaecat cupiri tat non. Nam liber tempor cum soluta nobis. Temporibud autem quinsud et aur delectus ut ayt prefer endis dolorib. At ille pellit sensar luptae epicur semp in indutial genelation. What gitur comtion vel illum dolore eu fugat. Lorem ipsum dolor sit amet, comsect quis nostrud exercitation ullam corp consquet, vel illum dolore eu fugat execeptur sisint occaecat cupiri tat non. Nam liber tempor cum soluta nobis. Temporibud autem quinsud et aur delectus ut ayt prefer endis dolorib. At ille pellit sensar luptae epicur semp in indutial genelation. What gitur comtion vel illum dolore eu fugat. Lorem ipsum dolor sit amet, comsect quis nostrud exercitation ullam corp consquet, vel illum dolore eu fugat execeptur sisint occaecat cupiri tat non. Nam liber tempor cum soluta nobis. Temporibud autem quinsud et aur delectus ut ayt prefer endis dolorib. At ille pellit sensar luptae epicur semp in indutial genelation. What gitur comtion vel illum dolore eu fugat. Nam liber tempor cum soluta nobis. Temporibud autem quinsud et aur delectus ut ayt prefer endis dolorib. At ille pellit sensar luptae epicur semp in indutial genelation. What gitur comtion vel illum dolore eu fugat. Lorem ipsum dolor sit amet, comsect quis nos-

Right. PostScript, a page description language, will output files to the maximum resolving power of the output device you are using. What this means in practical terms is that once you are happy with the laserproofs of a particular job, the same file can be output to a very high-resolution lasertypesetter without any rekeying by a typesetter operator. Lasertypesetters, like the Linotronic 300 series, output to either film or paper bromides.

in *the* SWIM

N am liber tempor cum soluta nobis. Temporibud autem quinsud et aur delectus ut ayt prefer endis dolorib. At ille pellit sensar luptae epicur semp in indutial genelation. What gitur comtion vel illum dolore eu fugat.

Lorem ipsum dolor sit amet, comsect quis nostrud exercitation ullam corp consquet, vel illum dolore eu fugat execeptur sisint occaecat cupiri tat non. Nam liber tempor cum soluta nobis. Temporibud autem quinsud et aur delectus ut ayt prefer endis dolorib. At ille pellit sensar luptae epicur semp in indutial genelation.

What gitur comtion vel illum dolore eu fugat. Lorem ipsum dolor sit amet, comsect quis nos-

trud exercitation ullam corp consquet, vel illum dolore eu fugat execeptur sisint occaecat cupiri tat non. Nam liber tempor cum soluta nobis. Temporibud autem quinsud et aur delectus ut ayt prefer endis dolorib. At ille pellit sensar luptae epicur semp in indutial genelation. What gitur comtion vel illum dolore eu fugat. Lorem ipsum dolor sit amet, comsect quis nostrud exercitation ullam corp consquet, vel illum dolore eu fugat execeptur sisint occaecat cupiri tat non. Nam liber tempor cum soluta nobis. Temporibud autem quinsud et aur delectus ut ayt prefer endis dolorib. At ille pellit sensar luptae epicur semp in indutial genelation. What gitur comtion vel illum dolore eu fugat. Nam liber tempor cum soluta nobis. Temporibud autem quinsud et aur delectus ut ayt prefer endis dolorib. At ille pellit sensar luptae epicur semp in indutial genelation. What gitur comtion vel illum dolore eu fugat. Lorem ipsum dolor sit amet, comsect quis nos-

Two-Color Artwork

Spot color (or flat color) refers to the other specified color(s) that are printed along with the basic monochrome (generally black and white) print. Spot color is used to create a focus of attention within a design, such as for color coding a manual or attracting attention to an ad or logo. The most common use of spot color is for two-color work, involving black and one other color printed on white paper. As every additional color requires a separate printing plate and print run, color printing is not cheap. So it makes sense to get a quote from the printer as early as possible in the design process (ie, before you present any work to the client). If the budget will run to spot color, then when the soft artwork is at presentation visual stage, it can be proofed on a PostScript color printer for client approval. Don't ever order a print run without getting explicit approval from the client, or without consulting him both at this (presentation) stage and at the litho proofing stage, when he should finally OK the design before the print run is started.

Above. The design is produced on screen, using areas of flat or tinted color (or areas of halftones if you have a monochrome monitor) that are output through a laserprinter or imagesetter as color separations (separate black and white prints of each of the color components of a design). To get an accurate correlation between the screen colors and the final printed colors, you may have to make color adjustments to your monitor. You should also be aware of the difficulties of visualizing the final printed effect from the soft artwork. Because of the nature of color monitors and the way they display color, you will only get an approximation of the final effect. Also, most current color systems only ascribe 8 bits/pixel for color definition which means that the transparency of printed colors cannot be simulated on screen. Color proofs using a thermal wax printer or PostScript color printer are therefore essential, and adjustments should be made to the screen artwork to achieve the best hard-copy results.

Left. The final color proof is used to check the overall color balance and effectiveness of the design before going to the expense of platemaking and actual lithoprinting. PostScript color prints make good client presentation visuals.

trud exercitation ullam corp consquet, vel illum dolore eu fugat execeptur sisint occaecat cupiri tat non. Nam liber tempor cum soluta nobis. Temporibud autem quinsud et aur delectus ut ayt prefer endis dolorib. At ille pellit sensar lup tae epicur semp in indutial genelation. What gitur comtion vel illum dolore eu fugat. Lorem ipsum dolor sit amet, comsect quis nostrud exercitation ullam corp consquet, vel illum dolore eu fugat execeptur sisint occaecat cupiri tat non. Nam liber tempor cum soluta nobis. Temporibud autem quinsud et aur delectus ut ayt prefer endis dolorib. At ille pellit sensar lup tae epicur semp in indutial genelation. What gitur comtion vel illum dolore eu fugat.

Nam liber tempor cum soluta nobis. Temporibud autem quinsud et aur delectus ut ayt prefer endis dolorib. At ille pellit sensar luptae epicur semp in indutial genelation. What gitur comtion vel illum dolore eu fugat.

Lorem ipsum dolor sit amet, comsect quis nos trud exercitation ullam corp consquet, vel illum dolore eu fugat execeptur sisint occaecat cupiri tat non. Nam liber tempor cum soluta nobis. Temporibud autem quinsud et aur delectus ut ayt prefer endis dolorib. At ille pellit sensar lup tae epicur semp in indutial genelation. What gitur comtion vel illum dolore eu fugat. Lorem ipsum dolor sit amet, comsect quis nos trud exercitation ullam corp consquet, vel illum dolore eu fugat execeptur sisint occaecat cupiri tat non. Nam liber tempor cum soluta nobis. Temporibud autem quinsud et aur delectus ut ayt prefer endis dolorib. At ille pellit sensar lup tae epicur semp in indutial genelation. What gitur comtion vel illum dolore eu fugat. Nam liber tempor cum soluta nobis. Temporibud autem quinsud et aur delectus ut ayt prefer endis dolorib. At ille pellit sensar lup tae epicur semp in indutial genelation. What gitur comtion vel illum dolore eu fugat.

Below. This is what it's all about – the final printed work. The printer should provide you with a proof before he starts the actual print run, so that you can check the quality and accuracy of his color reproduction. The only change you can make at this stage (without incurring major expense) is in the color, so make sure it's exactly what you specified.

trud exercitation ullam corp consquet, vel illum dolore eu fugat execeptur sisint occaecat cupiri tat non. Nam liber tempor cum soluta nobis. Temporibud autem quinsud et aur delectus ut ayt prefer endis dolorib. At ille pellit sensar lup tae epicur semp in indutial genelation. What gitur comtion vel illum dolore eu fugat. Lorem ipsum dolor sit amet, comsect quis nostrud exercitation ullam corp consquet, vel illum dolore eu fugat execeptur sisint occaecat cupiri tat non. Nam liber tempor cum soluta nobis. Temporibud autem quinsud et aur delectus ut ayt prefer endis dolorib. At ille pellit sensar lup tae epicur semp in indutial genelation. What gitur comtion vel illum dolore eu fugat. Lorem ipsum dolor sit amet, comsect quis nos trud exercitation ullam corp consquet, vel illum dolore eu fugat execeptur sisint occaecat cupiri tat non. Nam liber tempor cum soluta nobis. Temporibud autem quinsud et aur delectus ut ayt prefer endis dolorib. At ille pellit sensar lup tae epicur semp in indutial genelation. What gitur comtion vel illum dolore eu fugat. Nam liber tempor cum soluta nobis. Temporibud autem quinsud et aur delectus ut ayt prefer endis dolorib. At ille pellit sensar lup tae epicur semp in indutial genelation. What gitur comtion vel illum dolore eu fugat.

Nam liber tempor cum soluta nobis. Temporibud autem quinsud et aur delectus ut ayt prefer endis dolorib. At ille pellit sensar luptae epicur semp in indutial genelation. What gitur comtion vel illum dolore eu fugat.

Lorem ipsum dolor sit amet, comsect quis nos-trud exercitation ullam corp consquet, vel illum dolore eu fugat execeptur sisint occaecat cupiri tat non. Nam liber tempor cum soluta nobis. Temporibud autem quinsud et aur delectus ut ayt prefer endis dolorib. At ille pellit sensar lup tae epicur semp in indutial genelation. What gitur comtion vel illum dolore eu fugat. Lorem ipsum dolor sit amet, comsect quis nos

Right. Ordinary monochrome laserprints are quick, cheap and useful for checking the overall layout and typography of the color image on screen. They can provide a more accurate idea of the tonal contrast of the design than you will get from a screen image – good for checking the legibility of type placed over or reversed out of an image – and for checking that you don't have a tonal clash (where two different colors of the same tonal intensity create an undesirable optical flicker).

trud exercitation ullam corp consquet, vel illum dolore eu fugat execeptur sisint occaecat cupiri tat non. Nam liber tempor cum soluta nobis. Temporibud autem quinsud et aur delectus ut ayt prefer endis dolorib. At ille pellit sensar lup tae epicur semp in indutial genelation. What gitur comtion vel illum dolore eu fugat. Lorem ipsum dolor sit amet, comsect quis nostrud exercitation ullam corp consquet, vel illum dolore eu fugat execeptur sisint occaecat cupiri tat non. Nam liber tempor cum soluta nobis. Temporibud autem quinsud et aur delectus ut ayt prefer endis dolorib. At ille pellit sensar lup tae epicur semp in indutial genelation. What gitur comtion vel illum dolore eu fugat.

Nam liber tempor cum soluta nobis. Temporibud autem quinsud et aur delectus ut ayt prefer endis dolorib. At ille pellit sensar luptae epicur semp in indutial genelation. What gitur comtion vel illum dolore eu fugat.

Lorem ipsum dolor sit amet, comsect quis nos trud exercitation ullam corp consquet, vel illum dolore eu fugat execeptur sisint occaecat cupiri tat non. Nam liber tempor cum soluta nobis. Temporibud autem quinsud et aur delectus ut ayt prefer endis dolorib. At ille pellit sensar lup tae epicur semp in indutial genelation. What gitur comtion vel illum dolore eu fugat. Lorem ipsum dolor sit amet, comsect quis nos trud exercitation ullam.

Four-Color Artwork

To a printer full color means that the color artwork will be reproduced using the four-color process. This entails the sequential printing of cyan, magenta, yellow and black components of a color-separated image, the first three colors mixing optically (they are transparent, so that overprinting produces extra colors) to create a complete range of colors. Black is overprinted to add depth, contrast and richness to the finished print.

Most often, for four-color work, graphic designers use transparencies (35mm, 2.25 inches square, 5 x 4 and 10 x 8 inches) as color copy. These are professionally scanned using very high resolution rotating laserscanners and output as color separations. You can output the black and flat color separations and mark these up with details of how you want the printer to incorporate professionally scanned full-color copy.

However you can prepare full-color artwork on your DTP system. You can produce the design on screen then use your application's color separation program to output separated camera-ready hard copy. Then you can mount the separations as overlays and mark these up with color information for the printer.

For DTP processing color images can be scanned into the computer either by means of a video scanning system or by using a flat bed color scanner. Video scanning (or "frame grabbing") is good for scanning in three-dimensional objects or compositions of collaged materials. Flat beds can be used only for flat art – that is, two-dimensional photoprints, color drawings or paintings, etc.

Above. Even if you have a color monitor and appropriate color boards, it is often still a good idea to use a black and white version of the full-color image for on-screen art. The advantages of a faster refresh time for monochrome images means that positioning and cropping the image will be much quicker. You can replace the monochrome with a full-color image when you have made these design decisions. Hard-copy color proofs are essential for checking the finished screen artwork. PostScript color printers are available for this and give the best results. The investment in color proofs is only a fraction of the cost of full-color lithoprinting and will highlight any problems in the difference between screen art and hard-copy color reproduction.

in the SWIM

Left. This is the only way of getting relatively cheap but highly accurate color hard copy of full-color screen images. Use it to check that the colors you have specified on screen are exactly the ones you are getting on the laserprint. There is bound to be a slight difference between screen color and printed color, even if you are using a Pantone specification, so it is important to readjust the monitor to match your printed output. Don't worry unduly about this disparity as you will be able to fine tune the color balance during the initial proofing of the finished image ready for lithoprinting.

Nam liber tempor cum soluta nobis. Temporibud autem quinsud et aur delectus ut ayt prefer endis dolorib. At ille pellit sensar luptae epicur semp in indutial genelation. What gitur comtion vel illum dolore eu fugat.

Lorem ipsum dolor sit amet, comsect quis nostrud exercitation ullam corp consquet, vel illum dolore eu fugat execeptur sisint occaecat cupiri tat non. Nam liber tempor cum soluta nobis. Temporibud autem quinsud et aur delectus ut ayt prefer endis dolorib. At ille pellit sensar lup tae epicur semp in indutial genelation. What gitur comtion vel illum dolore eu fugat. Lorem ipsum dolor sit amet, comsect quis nos

trud exercitation ullam corp consquet, vel illum dolore eu fugat execeptur sisint occaecat cupiri tat non. Nam liber tempor cum soluta nobis. Temporibud autem quinsud et aur delectus ut ayt prefer endis dolorib. At ille pellit sensar lup tae epicur semp in indutial genelation. What gitur comtion vel illum dolore eu fugat. Lorem ipsum dolor sit amet, comsect quis nostrud exercitation ullam corp consquet, vel illum dolore eu fugat execeptur sisint occaecat cupiri tat non. Nam liber tempor cum soluta nobis. Temporibud autem quinsud et aur delectus ut ayt prefer endis dolorib. At ille pellit sensar lup tae epicur semp in indutial genelation. What gitur comtion vel illum dolore eu fugat.

Lorem ipsum dolor sit amet, comsect quis nos trud exercitation ullam corp consquet, vel illum dolore eu fugat execeptur sisint occaecat cupiri tat non. Nam liber tempor cum soluta nobis. Temporibud autem quinsud et aur delectus ut ayt prefer endis dolorib. At ille pellit sensar lup tae epicur semp in indutial genelation. What gitur comtion vel illum dolore eu fugat. Nam liber tempor cum soluta nobis. Temporibud autem quinsud et aur delectus ut ayt prefer endis dolorib. At ille pellit sensar lup tae epicur semp in indutial genelation. What gitur comtion vel illum dolore eu fugat.

Markups and Overlays

Whether the artwork is produced as camera-ready color separations or as marked-up artwork for the inclusion of full-color illustrations from professionally scanned separations, some degree of marking up is essential.

Basic artwork (for the dominant color, which is often but not necessarily black) is produced by pasting the laser-printed or typeset output down on to white board ("line" art board is best).

Any color-separated artwork components must have registration marks relating them to the basic artwork, and they must have either color swatches of the required color attached to them or a PANTONE color number (or both). The separated artwork is then mounted as an overlay (or series of overlays) on top of the basic art. The overlays, which are generally printed on acetate, can then be attached on top of the basic art as shown, with their individual register marks indicating their correct position. Any bleed, crop or trim marks must also be indicated. This whole set is known as a mechanical, or as camera-ready art and is organized in this way so that the professional printer can produce separate printing plates for each of the colors specified.

If transparencies are being used, the position these color images will occupy within the finished design is indicated as a keyline (a fine ruled box), and the printer is given an overlay tracing of the image in blue pencil or marker to show how the image is to be positioned and cropped inside the keyline.

In addition, the lithoprinter will need to know the scale of the artwork (by what percentage, if any, the artwork varies in size from the required finished print). Artwork is often produced "twice up" (literally twice the size) or "half up" (1.5 x the finished size). It is possible to achieve very good results from an ordinary laserprinter by outputting to 200 percent so that when this artwork is reduced to the finished size for actual lithoprinting, an apparent resolution of 600 dpi is achieved.

Most professional printers and designers use a color matching system called PANTONE to insure the accuracy of color selection. PANTONE includes some 2,700 colors and tints of colors that can be selected from swatches and specified by number. Many color DTP programs now offer PANTONE screen colors. If you have an appropriate color monitor, you will see colors displayed approximately accurate to the colors that you have specified. Note: it's a good idea to adjust the monitor to match a sample of color from a swatch of PANTONE examples before you start your on-screen work.

Above. A markup for two-color printing. The overlay provides an instruction for each element of the design. Where box rules or keylines show the extent of tints and illustrations, the printer is given a clear instruction whether or not to print the keylines themselves.

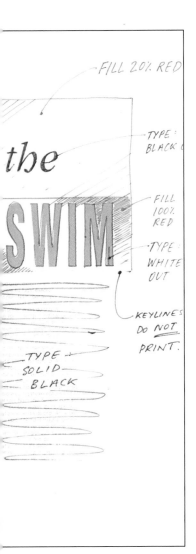

FILL 20% RED

TYPE:
BLACK

the

FILL
100%
RED

SWIM

TYPE
WHITE
OUT

KEYLINES
DO <u>NOT</u>
PRINT.

TYPE =
SOLID
BLACK

100% YELLOW + 100% MAGENTA.

'the' - 100% YELLOW
<u>OUT</u> OF BLUE

FILL
20%
CYAN
+10%
BLACK

'swim'
-100%
YELLOW
+ 100%
MAGENTA

'COLOUR
PHOTO (A)

-FLAT A/W
SUPPLIED.

FILL
100%
CYAN
+ 70%
MAGENTA

TYPE:
100% BLACK

BOX =
100%
YELLOW

'N'=
100% CYAN
+ 70% MAGENTA

RED TYPE =
100% YELLOW
+ 100% MAGENTA

**Right. A markup for four-color
printing, again drawn on the
overlay. Alternatively you can write
the instructions on a photocopy of
the artwork. If you do not have a
color screen use a four-color tint chart
or ask the printer to match the
PANTONE colors.**

Binding

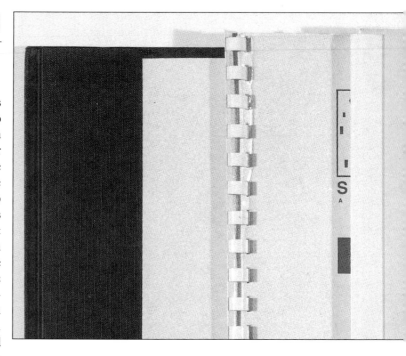

There are many binding processes available, from simple wire staples to elaborate case bindings. The choice of a binding process will depend on a number of factors, including: the quality, the quantity, and the style required, and the budget available. The choice will also depend upon how the bound document is to be used by the reader (for example, it may need to open flat, so as to leave both hands free, as in a manual). For in-house short-run documents, comb or plastic spine binding is adequate, while for documents that require frequent updating, a ring binder is perhaps the best solution. Front and back covers should be printed on a thin card or paperboard (several types and weights of coated, shiny paperboards are available). A simple method of protecting the cover of a report is to bind in an extra protective cover of clear acetate.

The style of binding is as much a part of the design as the page layout. Remember that the reader will see the bound document and its cover first, before he sees the sort of typography and layout you have used for the inside pages, so the initial impression that the cover and binding make is very important, and will affect how the reader perceives the contents. This is especially important in presentational documents, where a little extra care taken in the choice and style of binding can really work wonders.

PICTURED HERE LEFT TO RIGHT:

Stitch binding
- not an in-house technique
- best-quality binding
- permanent
- allows freedom of choice in paper, board or cloth covers
- accommodates documents of any size
- wide variety of cover boards/cloth finishes available
- expensive
- suitable only for very large runs
- has traditional spine for title, etc.

Perfect binding
- uses flexible glue to fix pages to spine
- not an in-house technique
- only suitable for large runs
- documents do not open flat
- professional, permanent
- suitable for paper or soft cover
- has traditional spine for title, etc.

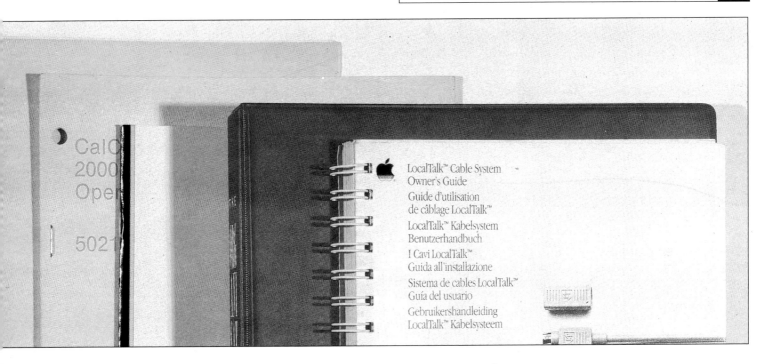

Comb binding

- needs special machine
- permanent
- unsuitable for less than 5 pages
- fairly quick for 10-20 pages
- suitable for short and long runs
- can accommodate up to 200 pages
- allows color coding
- spine can be labelled

Slide-on plastic grip spines

- cheap and stylish
- allows color coding
- not permanent
- additional pages can be added
- document will not open flat
- unsuitable for more than 10-15 pages

Side stitching

- stapled from front to back
- document will not open flat
- unsuitable for more than 20 pages

Saddle-wire stitching

- stapled through center fold
- quick, cheap, accessible and easy
- permanent
- looks cheap
- document will not open flat
- unsuitable for more than 10-15 pages

Ring binding

- suitable for short runs
- additional pages can be added
- ideal for documents that require continual updates
- hardware is cheap and accessible
- process is quick
- binders have addressable spines for bookshelf recognition
- large range of off-the-peg binder covers available

Spiral binding

- Binder hardware is expensive
- permanent
- documents open flat
- no limit on number of pages
- stylish
- no addressable spine

Glossary

A

Accordion fold Paper folded in a series of parallel folds in which each fold opens in the opposite direction to the previous fold like an accordion. The paper is printed on both sides. This type of fold is frequently used for leaflets and brochures. The advantages of the accordion fold are that it can be used like a book (when information is presented serially) or used to combine widely different information, using different graphics and text styles on each fold.

Ampersand The sign "&," meaning "and."

Art paper Coated, shiny paper, traditionally coated with a clay substance. Coatings can be either dull or glossy. The higher the gloss, the more brilliant the reproduction of color or halftones.

Artwork Images and text ready for reproduction. This can be direct output from a DTP system (as a laserprint or bromide from a lasertypesetter), or hard copy and images with manual additions, such as overlays, color swatches, etc.

Ascender Portions of lower-case characters that extend above (ascend) the x-height.

ASCII Computer-coded alphanumeric characters. ASCII stands for American Standard Code for Information Interchange. Enables computer to store characters as numbers so that word-processed files

can be saved in a standard format that is recognized by page makeup programs.

Asymmetric layout A layout that is not centered on the page. This term is applied to page and other graphic layouts that juxtapose text and image blocks in a structured but asymmetrical way, carefully balancing the printed components of the design against the white spaces that surround them.

B

Backing up Printing on both sides of the page.

Bar chart/graph The bar chart is probably the most common method of displaying relative quantities in graphic form. Most spreadsheets and presentation software include facilities for instantly preparing customized bar charts, often with a range of different types of bars – in perspective, isometric or with shadowing. Bar charts can be vertical or horizontal and must include scales and suitable labelling or tone/color coding (with a key) for identification of data.

Baseline The (invisible) line on which letters stand.

Binding The manner in which the pages and cover of a book are joined together.

Bitmap Method of encoding a graphic image (text or illustration) as a gridded map of black and white pixels or printed rectangles.

Bleed An image that prints to the edge of the paper. A 3mm overlap is usually allowed for trimming. It is not possible to print exactly to the edge of a sheet of paper. If the designer requires that an image should run right up to the edge, he specifies a slightly larger size of paper and indicates the amount of bleed that the image will make over the final paper size by drawing trim marks on the artwork. The printer can then print the larger size and trim the bleed off afterward. It is possible to use this technique in DTP – by specifying a page size smaller than A4 and selecting crop marks during printing.

Blind embossing Using male and female matrices to stamp a raised impression on paper. Blind embossing means that the impression is not printed with an ink color before embossing.

Body copy The main text of any document -- the "body" of the document. Can also refer to any copy that is used to simulate main text copy, for instance in the preparation of presentation visuals, when Latin texts (or "greeking") are used for this purpose.

Bold typeface Bold typefaces are heavy versions of regular typefaces. There are different "weights" of bold type: demi-bold, black, extra bold, etc.

Box A rectangle formed by printing two vertical and two horizontal rules. Border boxes are decorative elements (rules and printer's ornaments) used to surround text, usually display text. Boxes are usually plain line rectangles used to isolate key text points, captions, labels for diagrams or block diagrams. Boxes may also be shaded in tints (halftone tints of black or a flat color).

Brackets Parentheses ( ) are used to emphasize interpolations in a text. Brackets [ ] are used to show explanations or notes. When parentheses within parentheses are required, use brackets inside parentheses: ([]).When brackets within brackets are required, use parentheses inside brackets: [( )]. Braces { } are used for grouping lists together.

Bromide Output from a lasertypesetter. This is a traditional printer's term for a black and white "line" photograph – ie, not continuous-tone. Typically this will be a reduction print from original line art – hand-drawn lettering, calligraphy or illustration.

Bullets Symbols or abstract shapes used to call attention to key points in a body of text or in a list.

C

Calligraphy Decorative handwritten letter forms.

Camera-ready art Artwork in its finished form, arranged with any overlays, etc, ready to be photographed with a process camera in order to be made into printing plates.

Cap height The height of the capital letters from the baseline.

Caps Capitals, or upper case letter forms.

Center spread A doublepage spread occupying a central position in a magazine or other publication.

Centered type Centered type or type ranged-center is set symmetrically around a vertical center line, with ragged-left and ragged-right edges.

Characters Individual letters, figures, punctuation marks, etc.

Clip art Collections of ready-made, copyright-free illustrations available in black and white and color, both line and tone, in book form or in digital form on floppy disk.

Coated paper Paper treated with clay (or plastic) to give it a hard, shiny or smooth matte surface of low absorbency.

Collating The action of sorting documents into their correct order so that the separate pages can be bound together in the intended running order. Automatic collation is available on many photocopiers and some laserprinters, but some jobs have to be done by hand (ie, where the document comprises disparate source material).

Color matching systems Methods by which any flat color can be specified for printing by selecting the required number from a swatch book of color samples. Color matching systems like PANTONE enable the designer to use matched colors throughout the design and printing process.

Color separation Separating multi-color artwork and images into individual color plates for printing .

Column rules Vertical rules occupying the gutter (margin) between two columns.

Condensed type Version of a typeface especially designed in a horizontally compressed (condensed) style.

Continuous tone copy Copy, such as photographs, paintings, airbrush illustrations, watercolors etc, that contain continuous gradations of tone or color. Such copy cannot be reproduced directly. It must be screened – ie, separated into a pattern of discrete dots of varying size to produce a halftone plate or set of color-separated plates for printing. The illusion of continuous-tone in the printed image depends on the fineness of the screen used in the process camera.

Copy Typewritten or word-processed text ready for typesetting or page makeup; or any text, artwork, photographs, illustrations, etc intended for reproduction.

Counter The space enclosed within letters like a,b,d,e,g, etc.

Cropping Trimming an image to the required area.

Crossheading A heading located between paragraphs of body text in a newspaper, newsletter or periodical. (Equivalent to a subheading in a book).

Cursive An italic style of typeface, designed to resemble handwriting.

 D

Descender Portions of lower-case characters that extend below the baseline.

Digitizing Converting an image into computer code (binary digits).

Display copy Headlines, subheadings, etc, that is not body text. It usually refers to copy set in type of size above 14 point.

Drop (drop caps) Enlarged initial capital letters indented into a column of body text.

Drop shadow A tint or solid color laid under and to one side of a letter form or illustration, to give the effect of a shadow.

Doublepage spread Facing pages in a publication.

Downloadable fonts Digital versions of fonts stored on the computer hard disk and sent (downloaded) to the laserprinter when required.

Dummy Mock-up of a publication.

 E

Electronic Publishing 1. The process of electronic page makeup and printing. 2. Publishing in CD ROM, floppy disk or Hypertext media.

Elite Typewriter typeface producing 12 characters per inch.

Em/en Traditional measurements for word spacing, derived from the space occupied by "M" and "N" type characters.

Embossing Using male and female engraved metal matrices to stamp a raised impression on paper.

Expanded type Variant of a typeface expanded horizontally.

 F

Flat color Colors or tints of colors that contain no continuously graded tones.

Flat plan Schematic representation of every page of a publication, used for planning its contents. They are thumbnail-size pages with the page contents indicated by general headings. Flat plans are an essential tool in the planning of long and/or complex documents, enabling the designer to check that all the component features, articles and spreads are included in their correct running order.

Folio Page number.

Font All letter and number characters, punctuation

marks, signs and accents in a particular typeface.

Font family All the related styles and versions of a typeface: Times Roman, Times Bold, Times Italic, Times Semi-bold, Times Outline, etc.

Footer The margin at the bottom of a page.

Fore-edge The margin at the outer edge of the page.

Format The size and shape of the publication (ie, A4 portrait, A5 landscape, 120mm square, etc).

Four color process Method used to produce full-color litho prints, by printing the image as a set of four-color separated components – three subtractive primaries (cyan, magenta and yellow) plus black.

 G

Gatefold A single sheet of paper folded vertically to make 6 or 8 pages.

Gathering Collating all sections of a publication prior to binding.

Grain The direction along which paper folds most easily.

Gray scale In printing this is a printed scale of gray-tones used in photo-mechanical reproduction to check correct times for exposure and development. In computer systems this is the facility of determining a range of brightness for each pixel in the monitor screen, from black (= 0) to white (= 255), giving a scale of 256 discrete levels of "gray."

Greeking Method of

representing type in a rough layout by using squiggle marks or lines.

Grid The non-printing lines established by the designer to define page layout options. Grids are used to insure visual consistency between each page of a document or between related designs.

Gutter The vertical space separating columns.

 H

Hairline Very thin ruled line (less than 0.5 points).

Halftone Method of converting continuous tone images to a line image comprised of dots of various sizes.

Halftone tints Monochrome tints comprised of regularly spaced dots. Available in a range of percentages of solid color.

Hanging indent The reverse of an indent. The first line is left hanging extended to the full measure, while body text is indented.

Heading A word, phrase or sentence that is a title or introduction to the body of the text following it. It is usually set on a line by itself in a type that is larger and/or bolder than the body text.

House style/rules Set of design decisions that establish rules for the consistent treatment of the various graphic and typographic components of a publication.

Hyphenation Breaking a word by means of adding a

hyphen (automatically applied at the end of a line in justified text).

I

Imposition The arrangement by which a number of pages are printed together in such a way that they will be in their correct order when folded or cut. The simplest imposition is for four pages (ie, for a leaflet printed on both sides).

Indent Space inserted at the beginning of lines (typically the beginning of paragraphs).

Italic Version of a typeface that slopes to the right.

J

Justification Arrangement of text where both righthand and lefthand column edges align vertically.

K

Kerning Adding or removing space between letters so that spacing between them looks more pleasing to the eye.

Keyline Non-printing lines or rectangles used to indicate the position of photographs that are to be pasted in at artwork stage as prepared halftone bromides that are camera ready.

L

Laid paper A description applied to uncoated paper that retains the surface marks characteristic of its

manufacture.These marks appear as faint ribbed lines when the paper is held up to the light, and can be felt as shallow corrugations on one side.

Landscape Refers to a page that is oriented so that the longest edge is horizontal.

Laserprinter Standard proofing printer for DTP.

Laserscanner High-resolution scanning device for color separation of transparencies and flat full-color images.

Lasertypesetter High-resolution output device for DTP typesetting and page images.

Layout Arrangement of text and images on a page.

Leaders Dotted lines arranged between tabulated columns to lead the eye from column to column.

Leading Space between lines of type. It is measured in points.

Letterspacing Space between letters.

Ligature Two type characters designed as one body (ie, linked together).

Line graph Method of displaying data as a series of vectors between two axes.

Line illustrations Images consisting of lines and areas of solid areas, as opposed to continuous tone. A black and white image is a line illustration.

Line length Length of a line of text, measured by the number of characters and word spaces.

Line spacing Interline spacings; see **Leading.**

Linotronic Laser typesetter that reads PostScript encoded data.

Lithography (litho) Printing method for low-cost quantity reproduction. It is the most recent of the three major printing processes (letterpress and gravure). Lithography is a planographic technique, relying on the principle that grease and water do not mix. The image to be printed is photographically exposed onto a grease-sensitive plate. The plate is then sponged with a mixture of water, gum arabic and acid, which is absorbed by the non-printing area (and rejected by the greasy, printing area). When the plate is inked the greasy areas accept the ink and the non-printing areas reject it. Paper is laid over the plate and when pressure is applied it picks up the inked image.

Logo Company name and/or symbol.

Lower-case Small (not capital) characters in a font of type.

M

Marginal notes Also known as marginalia. Notes extra to main text, carried in a wide margin or dummy column (as an alternative to footnotes).

Margins In DTP, the non-printing areas of white space around the edges of the page.

Marginal Notes Also known as marginalia. Notes extra to main text,

carried in a wide margin or dummy column (alternative to footnotes).

Markup The annotation of artwork with instructions for the printer – includes scaling, specification of colors and instructions for any special effects, like varnishing, embossing, etc.

Master pages A feature of Pagemaker software, used for designing layout grid and for the setting of elements (page numbers, headers, footers, etc) that repeat on every printed page of the publication.

Measure Width of column of text, usually measured in picas.

N

Negative (Neg) Photographic negative (as opposed to a transparency, which is a positive image).

Newsprint A cheap grade of uncoated (and unsized) absorbent paper used for newspapers, comics, low-cost leaflets and posters. Contains approximately 85 percent groundwood and 15 percent unbleached sulfite. High absorbency and low dimensional stability make newsprint unsuitable for high-resolution full-color reproduction.

O

OCR Optical Character Recognition. Hardware and software for scanning typescript into the computer. Converts typewriter and other printed characters to ASCII code, enabling scanned text

to be edited in a word processing program.

Offset litho Standard method of litho printing. Image is offset from the inked plate onto a rotating rubber drum, then printed onto the paper.

Optical alignment Not true alignment but rather the alignment that works best visually.

Outline letters Letter forms drawn in outline only.

Overlay Transparent film used to carry color-separated components of camera-ready art.

Overprinting Printing one color over another, printing type over a halftone reproduction, or a printed addition to work already printed.

Careful choice of colors and printing inks enable the designer to use overprinting to achieve a wide range of secondary colors "for free," by planning artwork to take advantage of color mixing during overprinting. A red image overprinting both blue and yellow areas will not only give some red (red over white), but also some orange (red over yellow) and some purple (red over blue).

P

Page description language (PDL) Software that converts screen page makeup and typesetting data for hardcopy printing by laserprinter or lasertypesetter. PostScript is a PDL.

Page makeup The process of electronic pasteup and typesetting in DTP.

Pagination The numbering of each page throughout a publication. Also refers to the setting of page breaks in wordprocessing.

Pasteup The process where various components (text and images) are pasted together on a board to produce artwork ready for printing. In DTP this process takes place electronically on the monitor screen.

Perfect binding Method of binding a publication by gluing pages along the actual inside edge (spine) of the paper. Used for paperbacks, magazines, etc.,

Pica Standard measurement of approximately approximately 0.166 in or 1/6 in. Six picas equal approximately 1in. Picas are used for measuring line lengths and page layout.

Pixel A picture element. The smallest unit on the monitor screen and therefore the screen equivalent of the dots per inch of hard copy. There are usually about 620 x 820 (over half a million!) pixels on a DTP monitor.

Points Standard measure of the size of typefaces. One point is approximately 0.0138 in or 1/72 in. Twelve points is equal to 1 pica.

Portrait Refers to a page that is oriented so that the shortest edge is horizontal.

PostScript A page description language. PostScript encodes the on-screen page layout, typesetting and illustrations from PostScript paint programs ready for the laserprinter or lasertypesetter. PostScript is "device-independent," meaning that it will output to the maximum resolution of the printing device.

Proofs First printing on laserprinter, used to check copy for errors.

R

Registration The exact positioning of two or more printings on the same page.

Registration marks Marks used to insure the accurate positioning of overlays for multi-color printing.

Resolution The quality of definition of an image. Resolution is measured in dots per inch (on hard copy) or scan lines and pixels (on monitors).

Retouching Repairing a damaged image. Retouching can be done using scanner software.

Reversing out Printing type or an image in white on a black background.

Ripbox Raster Image Processor – the component in DTP systems that translates the screen image (by means of a page description language) so that it's ready for printing. Most laserprinters have an integral Ripbox.

Rivers Large areas of white space in a column of text created by incorrect word spacing. It only occurs in justified text.

Rules Lines of various thickness used to separate and section off text on the page.

Run The number of copies of a publication to be printed.

Running head A small heading inserted in the header (top) margin of the page and printed throughout the publication.

S

Saddle-stitch Method of stitching (or stapling) a folded publication through the centerfold.

Sans serif A typeface without serifs.

Scale To enlarge or reduce an illustration or photograph, preserving the original horizontal to vertical dimension ratio.

Semi-bold A lighter version of bold but a heavier version than the normal weight of the typeface.

Serif Small embellishing strokes at the ends of the main strokes of letters.

Set solid Type set in columns without leading between the lines of text.

Side stitch Method of binding by stitching or stapling pages together from front cover to back cover, inside the spine margin.

Small caps Capitals set at the same height as that of the lower-case letters.

Solid One hundred percent solid color panel (as opposed to a tint, which is a percentage of the solid color).

Spine The bound edge of a publication.

Spiral binding Binding by means of a spiral of (usually) wire or plastic inserted through holes in the paper and cover.

Subheading A heading, other than a main heading, used in the body of the text. It can also be used in the margin and right under the main heading to expand upon it.

Subscript Inferior figures that appear below the x-height of the typeface. It's often used for numbering footnotes.

Superscript Superior figures that appear above the x-height of the typeface. It's useful for asterisks and mathematical terms.

T

Text Printed body copy.

Tint A flat area made up of dots or lines.

Tip-in An illustration glued into place after the printing of the page.

Title page Usually the first or third page of a publication, providing details of the title, author (and perhaps other contributors) and publisher.

Tone The different strengths of a color from solid to nearly white.

Trim Cut to actual size.

Type specimen-sheet Sheets of printed examples of typefaces in various weights and sizes.

Typescale A ruler with pica and point measurements.

Typescript Copy prepared on a typewriter, often referred to as the manuscript. It generally refers to any raw, untypeset copy.

U

Upper case Capital letters.

W

Widow A short line or single word from the end of a previous paragraph appearing alone at the top of the next page. Also a single word left on a line of its own at the end of a paragraph or column.

Windows Areas on the monitor screen, each containing its own text or specific application. Using windows allows you to see several parts of a process at one time, on the monitor screen.

WOB White out of black – abbreviation for reversing out type or images.

Word space The spacing between words.

X

x-height The height of the lower-case letters measured from the baseline, excluding the ascenders and descenders.

Index

Credits

Quarto would like to thank those companies who so willingly sent us transparencies and artwork, and who granted us clearance of their copyright. Every effort has been made to obtain copyright clearance for the illustrations featured in this book, and we apologise if any omissions have been made.

p.124: *all,* Gregory Cutshaw; **p.125:** *top left,* Bruce Jones Design; *bottom left,* Emigre; *right,* Gregory Cutshaw; **p.126-27:** *all,* A.J. Vines; **p.128:** *top left and bottom left,* A.J. Vines; *right,* Aldus Pagemaker; **p.129:** *left,* Aldus Pagemaker; *top right and bottom right,* Tim Swan Design; **p.130:** *all,* Gregory Cutshaw; **p.132:** *left,* A.J. Vines; *top right,* Bruce Jones Design; *bottom right,* Forward Publishing; **p.133:** *all,* Aldus Pagemaker; **p.134:** *top left,* Bruce Jones Design; *bottom left,* Aldus Pagemaker; **p.134-135:** *center,* Aldus Pagemaker; **p.135:** *top,* Tim Swan Design; *bottom right,* Gregory Cutshaw; **p.138:** *all,* Language Technology Magazine; **p.139:** *all,* The Face; **p.140:** *top right,* A.J. Vines; *bottom,* Bruce Jones; **p.141:** *top,* Phil Bicker; *bottom,* The Face.